THE AFTERLIFE OF
THE 'SOVIET MAN'

Russian Shorts

Russian Shorts is a series of thought-provoking books published in a slim format. The Shorts books examine key concepts, personalities, and moments in Russian historical and cultural studies, encompassing its vast diversity from the origins of the Kievan state to Putin's Russia. Each book is intended for a broad range of readers, covers a side of Russian history and culture that has not been well-understood, and is meant to stimulate conversation.

Series Editors:

Eugene M. Avrutin, Professor of Modern European Jewish History,
 University of Illinois, USA
Stephen M. Norris, Professor of History, Miami University, USA

Editorial Board:

Edyta Bojanowska, Professor of Slavic Languages and Literatures,
 Yale University, USA
Ekaterina Boltunova, Associate Professor of History, Higher School of
 Economics, Russia
Eliot Borenstein, Professor of Russian and Slavic, New York University, USA
Melissa Caldwell, Professor of Anthropology, University of California, Santa
 Cruz, USA
Choi Chatterjee, Professor of History, California State University, Los
 Angeles, USA
Robert Crews, Professor of History, Stanford University, USA
Dan Healey, Professor of Modern Russian History, University of Oxford, UK
Polly Jones, Associate Professor of Russian, University of Oxford, UK
Paul R. Josephson, Professor of History, Colby College, USA
Marlene Laruelle, Research Professor of International Affairs, George
 Washington University, USA
Marina Mogilner, Associate Professor, University of Illinois at Chicago, USA
Willard Sunderland, Henry R. Winkler Professor of Modern History,
 University of Cincinnati, USA

Published Titles

Pussy Riot: Speaking Punk to Power, Eliot Borenstein
Memory Politics and the Russian Civil War: Reds Versus Whites, Marlene
 Laruelle and Margarita Karnysheva
Russian Utopia: A Century of Revolutionary Possibilities, Mark Steinberg
Racism in Modern Russia, Eugene M. Avrutin
Meanwhile, In Russia: Russian Memes and Viral Video Culture,
 Eliot Borenstein

Upcoming Titles

THE AFTERLIFE OF THE 'SOVIET MAN'

RETHINKING *HOMO SOVIETICUS*

Gulnaz Sharafutdinova

BLOOMSBURY ACADEMIC

LONDON • NEW YORK • OXFORD • NEW DELHI • SYDNEY

BLOOMSBURY ACADEMIC
Bloomsbury Publishing Plc
50 Bedford Square, London, WC1B 3DP, UK
1385 Broadway, New York, NY 10018, USA
29 Earlsfort Terrace, Dublin 2, Ireland

BLOOMSBURY, BLOOMSBURY ACADEMIC and the Diana logo are trade-marks of Bloomsbury Publishing Plc

First published in Great Britain 2023

Series design by Tjaša Krivec
Cover Image: Hi-Story © Alamy Stock Photo

A catalogue record for this book is available from the British Library.

A catalog record for this book is available from the Library of Congress.

ISBN: PB: 978-1-3501-6772-8
HB: 978-1-3501-6771-1
ePDF: 978-1-3501-6773-5
eBook: 978-1-3501-6774-2

Typeset by Deanta Global Publishing Services, Chennai, India
Printed and bound in Great Britain

To find out more about our authors and books visit www.bloomsbury.com and sign up for our newsletters.

CONTENTS

PROLOGUE

My beloved grandmother, Raisa Nurullovna Akhmetzyanova, will soon turn 98. She was born in a country that is not on the map anymore. Many people in the West would recognize the country through the combination of four letters – CCCP – that translates from Russian as USSR or the Union of Soviet Socialist Republics (the Soviet Union, for short). On her birthday, a congratulatory letter from the president of the Russian Federation, Vladimir Putin, made it to Chistopol (Tatarstan), the town she lives in now. Most of her life she lived in two nearby villages – Islyaikino and Kargali. From the passing of my grandfather in 1998, she lived alone until 2011, when her daughter joined her. They moved to a small town, Chistopol, just fifteen miles away from the village in 2013. The village amenities – the outside toilet and lack of running water – became too hard for her to endure. As a war veteran, she could get a small modern apartment in a nearby town.

The move was painful. She had to leave the house where she raised her four kids and cared for her grandkids on summer holidays. She left her social circle behind along with all material possessions. Only the most essential items made it to the new place along with the state medals, reward papers and old letters written by her children and grandchildren. Her social network did not disappear entirely. Some people were a phone call away; others could visit. Still, it took time and patience to adjust to the new place. Multiple daily prayers, those essential phone calls from relatives and remaining village contacts, the books from the local library in Tatar language, and the television – these are the remaining props that keep my grandma connected to social life.

For better or worse, life for my grandma had always been about a family and a community. Social expectations played a leading role in her perceptions and decision-making. Retiring at fifty-five, the last forty years of her life she continued to play a central role in the affairs of the extended family, always abreast of all the news, ready to praise or criticize, very judgemental, giving and hard-working, at least until the last few years, when her health issues interfered with her mobility and strength. This web of deep family and social connections that she created is undoubtedly one of the key foundations of her long life. Some recent studies in the West demonstrate the beneficial health effects of social ties and meaningful relationships. My grandma set high standards for all of her family in terms of how to be socially connected.

My grandmother is a simple Soviet woman born, raised, educated and having lived most of her life in the Soviet Union. She started working in the collective farm she lived in at the time of purges in the 1930s. She worked hard as a teenager and young woman before and during the war, quitting school after four years of elementary school. Marrying in 1942, she confronted the cruelty of the Stalinist system, as her newly wed husband was imprisoned for alleged 'theft of socialist property'. The case was later turned into a case of 'negligence'. The story goes that she was able to free him by bribing the judge in Kazan, the republican capital, where all the accused in relation to this case were taken for the trial and deportation to a more remote colony in the East. These events took place during November 1942 to February 1943. My grandmother was nineteen years old. She gave birth to her first son on 16 March 1943. My grandfather was eighteen at the time. He was freed and returned from Kazan in spring 1943. One month later he went to war, which he survived, only returning back in 1947. My father was born in 1948 and my two aunts in 1952 and 1954.

In contrast to my grandmother, whose stories filled my life, my grandfather never talked about war. Internalizing traumas, the way many Soviet men did and Russian men continue to do, he turned to alcohol. Drinking was a social problem in the Soviet Union. Alcoholism – not 'Soviet personality traits', as the well-known sociologist Yuri Levada claimed or totalitarian traits as George Orwell argued – was the main compensatory mechanism used by a 'simple Soviet man' to accommodate himself to the challenges of life.

It is etched in my memory how we, as kids, observed a daily drunk walk home by some villagers, on the street in Kargali. The number of broken lives and families due to alcoholism was colossal. Domestic violence, high male mortality rates and single-mother families were all tragic manifestations of problems with alcoholism. Rural life, in particular, presupposed a lot of drinking, but alcohol consumption was tolerated and even encouraged at work and at home – in cities as well. The Soviet authorities kept the price of vodka low. Soviet movies conveyed the social norms of drinking in classics such as *Moscow Does not Believe in Tears* (1980) and *The Irony of Fate* (1975).

More than sixty years later, in 2006, Raisa's granddaughter, Albina (born in 1971), my cousin and best childhood friend, freed her husband ('to be' at the time) from prison too, using similar methods and replaying the fate of her grandmother. 'Don't count out a prison cell, a begging bowl may come as well' states an old Russian proverb echoing a more neutral 'man proposes, God disposes'. Only in the Soviet Union it was not God. It was the state that constantly hovered over the lives of Soviet citizens.

Such state has been rebuilt in Russia. Vladimir Putin's leadership took the country away from the path it stepped on after the collapse of the Soviet Union. The beginning of Russia's military invasion of Ukraine on 24 February 2022 burnt the remaining bridges between Russia and the West. The last flicker of hope and promise of new Russia was obliterated with this unprovoked aggression that built on the pattern of revanchist politics the Kremlin stood on earlier. The revenge-driven geopolitics drowned the immediate present and future of the Russian society and economy in the troubling waters of uncertainty, isolation and degradation.

The reconstitution of the Russian state did not happen overnight. Over the last two decades we have witnessed a gradual rise of the Russian authoritarian regime that equated itself with the state and exerted a heavy-handed control over informational space erasing to the ground the spaces of autonomous social and political action, and civic activism. Russia's politics have turned more repressive and more aggressive towards the West and towards its own society. Along with this return, we saw the return of various ideas and terms that often turn into labels used by observers in and outside Russia to make sense of what they see or read about. These terms and ideas have history. They reflect politics. They reveal individual lives, choices and meanings.

This book investigates the origins and history of one such term – *Homo Sovieticus* – or the Soviet person. It is a term that could be used in relation to my grandmother, grandfather, my parents or my cousin. Born in 1973, I fit this term, too. Many of my generation would proudly declare today, 'I am a Soviet person'. It is a term that some people in present-day Russia would use with pride, identifying with the Soviet people and highlighting the dispositions and behaviours they associate with the past (i.e. sociality and friendship), and see as missing from their present. But many others would use the denigrating *sovok*, referring to people clinging to practices and attitudes associated with life in the Soviet Union. A small informal survey conducted in December 2021 by Ksenia Turkova, a journalist at the Voice of America, revealed the multiplicity of meaning contained in the term *sovok*. Many of her respondents understood it as a special mentality characterized by infantilism, closed mind and xenophobia; a combination of all negative behavioural and psychological traits associated with the legacy of living in poverty and fear in a repressive Soviet state.[1] Today, a newer term – *vatnik*, 'the grandson of the *sovok*' – is used in Russia as a common slur and a politicized label for those Russians who invoked aggressive pro-Putin patriotism.[2]

Similar to *sovok*, *Homo Sovieticus* is often (though not always) used as a stigmatizing term presumed to capture the imprint of totalitarianism and a Soviet way of life on Soviet people. No single set of attributes associated with *Homo Sovieticus* exists. Different intellectuals imbued the term with different meanings depending on their own experiences, political stance and disciplinary traditions, approaches and methodologies. The ideas about the Soviet man have shifted from white to black, from simple to complex, from good to evil and back. Nonetheless, the dominant meaning of *Homo Sovieticus* – the negative and stigmatizing one – was developed through the analytical lens of totalitarianism and the political stance of anti-communism. Its fullest and most empirically developed expression took place in the work of Yuri Levada and his colleagues. Their research project on

Soviet personality type highlighted the sense of Soviet exceptionalism, state paternalism, egalitarianism combined with deference to authority and imperial syndrome as key characteristics of the Soviet personality type. Masha Gessen relied on this particular notion of *Homo Sovieticus* in her recent, award-winning book *The Future Is History* (2017). Reviewing the book for the readers of the *New York Times* audience, Francis Fukuyama, a Stanford professor best known for his 'end of history' argument, summarized as follows the book's idea about what the Putin regime represents: 'an entire society psychologically damaged and unwilling to come to terms with its own past, leading to a widespread depression and belief that the country has no future'.[3]

This line of thinking has been re-emerging in the public sphere along with the growing anxiety about Russia's domestic and foreign policies after 2014. Russia's war against Ukraine is likely to dramatically reinforce these essentializing views of Russia, Russian history and even culture that have been on the rise even among the more insightful Russia observers, such as Thomas Graham, a former government official, who traced the contemporary issues with Russia to the value gap that presumably opened at the end of the Napoleonic era.[4] Russia's aggression against Ukraine bolsters views such as that, expressed in December 2021, by the US Deputy Secretary of State Victoria Nuland, who suggested that Vladimir Putin is harbouring plans to recreate the Soviet Union.[5] Since Putin is often viewed as a symbol of Russia and Russians, many of whom harbour feelings of Soviet nostalgia, discussed widely in the Western press, the overall puzzle of Russian politics gets resolved rather easily.[6] The Russian society is nostalgic for its glorious past and the Russian president is trying to bring it back. *Homo Sovieticus* then appears as the ultimate culprit of not only Russia's failed democratization but also of Russia's aggression against Ukraine.

Now, think about the political implications of the idea that Putin's regime represents the psychologically damaged society suffering from a post-totalitarian syndrome. Such labels might be easy to grasp: they offer simple answers. But who is there to deal with their aftermath? What do they mean for the ongoing political battle – visible or invisible – in Russia and for those who sacrifice their lives and freedom to bring about a different Russia? What do they mean for millions of others who might not be fighting the system but trying to live their lives in however imperfect ways, as we all do?

Ironically, those born and educated in the Soviet Union are often the first ones to reproduce the ideas associated with *Homo Sovieticus*. As Ilya Lozovsky lamented in his 2015 post: 'the legacy of growing up in a paranoid, undemocratic society remains'.[7] Leonid Bershidsky, a columnist at Bloomberg, shared in his op-ed dedicated to thirty-year anniversary of the Soviet break-up in December 2021:

> The shared experience of growing up under the low ceilings of drafty, indescribably ugly concrete boxes. The kindergartens and schools that prepared one for prison as much as for the factory or the sleepy research institute where our parents pretended to work for pretend pay. The ideologically correct movies that everyone watched in ceaseless re-runs. The punishing lines for everything one could buy and the never-ending quest for what one couldn't. The day-in, day-out submission, compromise and secret defiance. We post-Soviets can still see it all in each other's eyes. [. . .] We've brought the Soviet Union – hated or loved, as the case may be – with us. We don't live in what's left of it, but it lives on in us, in the cartoons we show our kids, the music we listen to, the books we quote, the prejudices we harbor.[8]

This book argues against such cosy but stigmatizing ideas being reproduced in contemporary public discourse. To support that argument, it looks at the term *Homo Sovieticus* through the selective stories about people who developed its various meanings. A product of intellectuals from different countries, the idea of *Homo Sovieticus* has always reflected these intellectuals' personal encounters with communism as well as their more deeply embedded cultural dispositions. The ideological, political and professional aspirations of many of these individuals developed during the Cold War and, therefore, reflect and helped to produce the politics of the Cold War. The geopolitical context of two opposing systems became reinscribed in human sciences in a simple binary vision: democracy and free markets produced free and autonomous liberal subject, while totalitarianism produced *Homo Sovieticus*, an enslaved, indoctrinated, illiberal man. In the next chapter I argue that the resonating comeback of such Cold War myths should be attributed to the most basic psychological processes that take place in a concrete geopolitical context but apply quite universally across different countries. The awareness of how our thinking patterns might work to bring back such old ideas is paramount today.

The academic community has long moved away from these notions. Historians, cultural theorists and sociologists have written volumes exposing the ideological and reductionist nature of many of such assumptions propagated in the context of the Cold War and replacing these images with the more complex ideas and more nuanced representations. Nonetheless, politics of geopolitical polarization and human psychology have coalesced, so that Russia's growing domestic authoritarianism and confrontational foreign policy led towards a resuscitation of the black-and-white images, making the Cold War-era thinking relevant once again.

This book is written in response to these developments and as a call for greater self-awareness and understanding of the terms we operate with in our daily life. The Kremlin had taken Russia in the wrong direction. It is the responsibility of the Russian citizens to pressure for political change and seek transformation, to repent over the criminal deeds of their government and support Ukraine and Ukrainians. However, this could only happen if the humanity of millions of Russians is not compromised with the use of simplified and stigmatizing labels and shortcuts that are ultimately rooted in politics and history. However painful the endeavour, however uncomfortable confronting people with different worldviews, we need not forget our common humanity.

CHAPTER 1
ON RIDING BICYCLES AND HUMAN JUDGEMENT

Sometimes we think fast; sometimes we think slow. The prominent psychologist and economist Daniel Kahneman has helped to popularize this difference and has explained why it happens (2011). It is in the nature of *Homo sapiens* to lean towards easy answers to difficult questions. We all tend to rely on well-flexed mental muscles and the habitual patterns of thinking because deliberation requires additional effort. You do not need to learn bicycle riding twice: the neural networks established in the process of learning work automatically and the process of riding is routinized and removed from our active awareness.

Political thinking is no exception. The judgements we form throughout our lives build on each other and on our previously developed habits of thought. We can easily lose sight of the forces that trigger the expression of certain ideas and attitudes. Only unexpected events that contain a strong element of surprise can motivate us to undergo more deliberative search for an explanation that is not automatically available to us. Even then, our cognitive predispositions tend to process the unexpected information in such a way that it fits in the pre-existing mental moulds.

The mental moulds we develop are often biased. We tend to be more empathetic to ourselves and our own kin and less sympathetic to outsiders. Social psychologists have long noticed this pattern and labelled it 'a fundamental attribution error' in human judgement. Individuals tend to overestimate the role of situational factors in their own behaviour, while underestimating the role of dispositional factors. They do the opposite when they judge the behaviour of others. It appears that we all tend to blame circumstances for things we do wrong (or fail to do right) and blame the inherent traits and dispositions (whether of a person, a group or a country), when we look at something done by others. This cognitive trait applies to various contexts and situations across various cultures.

The 'group-attribution error' is one of the common variations of this human bias. We make attributional judgements not only about individuals but entire groups. We make self-serving and self-enhancing evaluations by generating more favourable explanations for in-group members and less favourable about out-groups, judging entire groups based on a few representatives or applying emerging group stereotypes to individual representatives. All these biases have been explored in social psychology through numerous experiments. Studies of racism, sexism, nationalism and other forms of discriminatory stereotyping reveal that social and political judgement is wrought by persistent biases and misjudgement.

The revival of discussions about *Homo Sovieticus* in the context of contemporary Russia, particularly after the 2014 annexation of Crimea, is a sign of such biases and stereotypes born in the cognitive processes discussed earlier. The pre-existing mental moulds were available and handy for explaining the distressing news coming out of Russia. Have you not recently had plenty of chances to have – 'oh, those Russians' – cross your mind again, when reading about the cases of Novichok poisoning, hearing about another Sputnik (or Sputnik V, as in the case with the first registered in Russia vaccine against the coronavirus?) and, now, reading the distressing news about the tragic, horrifying war in Ukraine? Do these latest developments in Russia just confirm your earlier beliefs about the country and its people? The habitual stereotypes we all carry about others are like well-worn shoes – they are cosy and easy to slide in. New shoes require more time and effort to break in. But in the times of political stress and anxiety, old and cozy ideas become especially handy.

Homo Sovieticus as a concept

The term 'Soviet man' or *Homo Sovieticus* may be referred to as an ideal-type that presumes to capture the average, most typical features of those who lived through the Soviet experience of communism. As such, it functions as a shorthand term reflecting the behavioural and psychological effects of communism. While first applied to Soviet citizens, it is also used in the context of other post-communist countries in Eastern Europe.[1] The Latin translation – *Homo Sovieticus* – is closer to the Russian *Sovetskii chelovek* – a term that is more neutral in its gender connotations. Lev Gudkov, a well-known Russian sociologist and one of the strongest proponents of the term today, had once compared the term *Homo Sovieticus* to other, related adaptations such as *Homo economicus* and *Homo politicus. Homo economicus* – the rational and self-interested utility-maximizer – is a central agent in economics discipline. *Homo politicus* is Plato's and Aristotle's reference to human beings as political animal. 'It is a characteristic of man that *he alone has any sense of good and evil, of just and unjust*', observed Aristotle. While these two older terms expressed presumably universal features of human existence, *Homo Sovieticus* is a historically contingent discursive formation. In its most reputable sociological adaptation by Yuri Levada and the colleagues who continue his legacy at the Levada Center, *Homo Sovieticus* is a human by-product of Soviet totalitarianism.

Levada's conceptualization built on earlier thinking that linked politics and personality type. This earlier work was done after the Second World War in an effort to analyse the origins of fascism. The influential German philosopher Theodore Adorno and his colleagues developed a concept of 'the authoritarian personality' trying to identify individual-level psychological dispositions congruent with fascism. Such personality type was assumed to be formed in early childhood and to later grow into a set of attitudes about authority, hierarchy, sexuality and tradition forming an ideological inclination towards fascism (1950). In the 1970s and 1980s the Eastern European and Soviet dissidents enriched this line of thinking applying it to communist countries although their focus was on individual-level *effects* of communism (as opposed to the drivers of communism). Their critical observations about how the system shaped individual psychology and behaviour were grounded in their personal experiences and reflected their personal political views. Their critical ideas were fully embraced and, to an extent, nurtured in the West. These anti-communist dissidents turned into active players in the highly contested geopolitics of the Cold War. The stakes were very high. Some of them lost their lives having made their political choices; others ultimately left the field of politics preferring to dedicate their lives to pursuits in the literature and poetry.

Russia's choice of democracy and markets in the early 1990s made these earlier ideas about *Homo Sovieticus* moot and irrelevant. Sociologists in Russia, who set out to study the Soviet person using survey research in the late 1980s, expected the core Soviet traits to disappear with the changing political system. Some Western scholars did wonder whether the political culture and personality type associated with the communist period might interfere with the challenges of democratization and marketization. A comparative study published in the *Brookings Papers on Economic Activity* in 1992 explored the relevance of attitudinal (personality traits and culture related) and situational factors for economic behaviour. The authors found that situational factors and not those associated with lasting personality traits played a bigger role in determining popular behaviour. They concluded that it would be misleading to refer to *Homo Sovieticus* as a distinct human type.[2] Arguably, this was the dominant opinion during the first post-communist decade of the 1990s, when the concept of *Homo Sovieticus* was seen as a relic of the past. Russian sociologists in Yuri Levada group, who studied *Homo Sovieticus* through regular, large-scale surveys during 1989–92, also thought they were studying a dying, decomposing species.

Russia's return to authoritarianism occurred gradually, but surely. Vladimir Putin's long leadership paralleled with the return to the more familiar institutional design, where issues of government accountability are not addressed and societal agency is squashed. Years of intentional political engineering during the 2000s reactivated old ideas, practices and political structures. Neither many Russian intellectuals critical of Putin's regime nor Russian observers in the West and the Western public could easily comprehend and make sense of the broad public euphoria in Russia with regard to the annexation of Crimea in 2014. As Putin's popularity ratings skyrocketed, those, perplexed by these developments, reacted by turning to *Homo Sovieticus*: the only way to understand this mood, it seemed, was to see Russians as post-Soviet citizens damaged by years of living under communism.

Sociologists from the Levada Center and, especially, Lev Gudkov have been the most crucial proponents of this idea in contemporary Russia.[3] Their surveys examining a 'Soviet simple man' continued throughout the 1990s and 2000s and turned into the main justification for claims that the Soviet man is still well and alive in Russia. The continuation of their surveys brought new revelations: a few decades after the Soviet collapse, the Soviet man was alive! 'Sovyetskii chelovek [Soviet person] has somewhat changed. He's been fed, he's changed his clothes, he's bought a car and owns a home. But he still feels insecure and vulnerable. And he's just as aggressive toward his neighbor', wrote Lev Gudkov, director of the Levada Center, in 2017 sharing the findings of Levada's surveys conducted over the preceding three decades.[4]

The reincarnation of soviet mentality and the Soviet man in Putin's Russia has been a subject of numerous debates since 2014, including those held at such reputable intellectual centres as the Sakharov Center, Carnegie Moscow Center and other public forums and media venues.[5] Some Russian commentators have even suggested that the Putin-era person appears more Soviet than she was during the Soviet era.[6] Even Vladimir Putin shared his, somewhat ambiguous, views about the concept of Soviet man at his Valdai speech in October 2021.[7] Paraphrasing Karl Marx, 'the spectre of homo sovieticus is haunting Russia.'[8]

Perhaps it was to be expected that the mental moulds and models created during the Cold War might experience a public return in the West as well as in Russia, as the Russian government moved in the direction of new authoritarianism and anti-Westernism. After all, as the earlier discussion about the old shoes went, we all like to see the familiar and ignore or defend against the strange and unrecognizable. Yet there are other ways of seeing and thinking about these issues, too. 'We're nostalgic but we're not crazy', stated the title of Serguei Oushakine 2007 article, in which Princeton anthropologist inquired into the process of retrofitting new artistic ideas into the old forms and shapes (2007). The old aesthetic shapes from the Soviet past are being reclaimed in the new context with new meanings. This artistic production inspired by the Soviet era and reflecting creativity and originality co-existed over the past years with the less original re-actualization of old tropes and meanings to make sense of current social and political developments. The war will undoubtedly drain the Russian cultural sphere of its more original and creative forms and meanings. However, as Irina Prokhorova (the founder, editor and publisher of the *New Literary Observer*) noted in her 2022 interview with Ekaterina Gordeeva, the Soviet experience tells us that cultural products never go waste: they get recovered and find use when the appropriate time comes.[9]

Creators of *Homo Sovieticus*

Any term, theory and logical construct has an analyst (in fact, many of them) behind it. An analyst and an observer who developed a specific vision of the reality, collected the facts, and advanced an interpretation of what stands behind those facts and how to make sense of them. Often, understanding the context in which that analyst lived, the challenges that analyst faced and aspirations she had can bring us to the place where we can comprehend the driving forces and the deeper sources of the type of selection and interpretation of facts offered by the analyst.

This book invites you to take a journey into the lives and works of writers, journalists, philosophers and scientists who advanced the construct of *Homo Sovieticus*. Each of the outstanding individuals discussed in this book deserves volumes written about them. Indeed, there are books written about some and will likely be written about others, too. They developed very different outlooks on *Homo Sovieticus*. Some took a one-sided, critical and judgemental stance equating Soviet individuals with the detested communist system. Others took a more empathetic and discerning approach driven by the desire to understand life under communism from the inside. These different outlooks reflect varying personal stories, vulnerabilities and different historical times shaping general sensibilities and the more specific ideas about *Homo Sovieticus*.

This journey is, by necessity, very selective. Many more writers and scholars who contributed to the study of the Soviet society and communist systems could be included in this book. No such selection could be free from arbitrariness and I can only hope that there will be other authors and books who could bring attention to different intellectuals and their lives and ideas. I tried to select my heroes to represent different times and different places they lived and created in. Some of them are very well known, others – less so. But all of them fit into one of the categories along which this book is organized and represent a case of either how *Homo Sovieticus* was understood by dissenting intellectuals in Eastern Europe and Soviet Union, how it was studied during the Soviet perestroika or how it was re-imagined after the fall of the Soviet Union.

During the 1940–1950s, communist systems were established in Poland, Czechoslovakia, Bulgaria, Hungary, East Germany, Romania, Yugoslavia and Albania. The Red Army liberated most of these from the Nazis, allowing Stalin to assert Soviet control over these territories at the end of the war. After the war, these states underwent forced radical transformations of their political, economic and social systems following the Soviet model of governance. The reputation of the Soviet Union was high after the war. In many cases, Soviet authorities could rely on the active collaboration of those who believed in communism and who wanted to find alternative solutions to economic and social problems that had accumulated in their societies. Communism seemed to provide such alternatives. Not only Eastern European but even American intellectuals and white-collar employees could hold strong pro-Soviet views. In his recent memoir, Peter Reddaway, a well-known scholar of Soviet politics, refers to his meeting in 1962 with an American attorney who was 'a devoted supporter of the Stalinist Communist Party' (Reddaway 2020: 29).

Nonetheless, the building of new, Soviet-like institutions in Eastern Europe was also accompanied by violence and the suppression of civil society. Those who disagreed with the institutional changes undertaken after the war were simply crushed. In her voluminous

The Iron Curtain (2012), the journalist Anne Applebaum tracked the work of Soviet operators in Eastern Europe during the process of establishing Moscow dictate. They persecuted and then banned all the independent institutions and rival political parties and groups. Some members of the cultural elite in these societies who could not adjust to new social and political expectations and opposed collaborating with the regime were able to escape to other countries after having experienced the repressive system for some time. Usually, these individuals, who were able to share their critical observations about how the system operated and how it impacted people, belonged to the intellectual elite. Having experienced the post-war transformation first-hand, they could explore the psychological consequences of living under the communist regime and the moral compromises people had to accept, if they were to adapt to the new system. Their observations became an early foundation on which the negative connotations of *Homo Sovieticus* later developed.

The political émigré writers dissenting against communism advanced the first critical analytical lens on the effects of communism on these societies. Opposing the new institutions and practices that came to dominate their lives, they questioned the impact of these institutions on individuals who lived in these conditions. Contrary to the utopian conception of the New Soviet Man that Bolsheviks wanted to bring into reality, thus emerged the new idea of *Homo Sovieticus* as a real, and less-than-appealing product of the totalitarian regime. Such recognition of the system's effects on human consciousness and psychology was articulated first in Eastern European countries – the Soviet satellites where communism was imposed from the outside. Such imposition resulted in an unavoidable clash with nationalistic sentiments, traditions and values.

The post-war Soviet Union also witnessed the rise of dissent. As in Eastern European countries, Soviet dissent emerged for the most part in intellectual circles. The Khrushchev-period and its cultural thaw in the 1950s and 1960s worked to open up some breathing spaces for creative professions and intellectual life. Thus, Aleksandr Solzhenitsyn's famous 'One Day in the Life of Ivan Denisovich', that described the ordinary day of an ordinary person imprisoned in a Soviet labour camp was published in 1962. The Thaw period was very brief and ended with the Sinyavsky-Daniel trial in 1966, when two Soviet writers were convicted for their literary satire on Socialist realism. Historians often see this trial as the beginning of the Soviet dissident movement.

The forced departure of selected Soviet dissenters to the West during the 1970s was one of the regime reactions to this movement. Such departure of critical intellectuals abroad, into emigration, left an unfillable void among their friends and colleagues at home. Reacting to these processes, Lev Kopelev, a Soviet writer and a dissident, compared the cultural landscape of Soviet society in the 1970s to 'a moonscape strewn with sterile, cavernous craters or gaps left behind by the flight of emigrants' (Zaslavsky 1994: 19).

It is during the brief opening of the Thaw that Yuri Levada, a Soviet sociologist who did not fit easily into the Marxist-Leninist tradition, developed his unorthodox views relying on the latest theoretical advancements in American sociology. Alas, he had to wait until Gorbachev's reforms in the second half of the 1980s to actualize his academic views and act on his professional aspirations that he referred to as the 'pursuit of the person'. But his intellectual work and leadership contributed the most to grounding the concept of *Homo Sovieticus* empirically and methodologically. When given his chance in the 1980s, Levada was certain that the Soviet man was a dying species. When the continuing opinion surveys revealed the same patterns of attitudes in post-Soviet Russia, sociologists were surprised: wasn't a Soviet person expected to disappear from the historical stage? Rather than rethinking the category and its foundations, they decided to stick to the term. The empirical observations from their surveys continued to prop the vision of *Homo Sovieticus* they constructed in the last years of Soviet life. The initial expectations of a radical transformation of the country's human material did not hold. Levada sociologists found themselves in the same place as early Bolsheviks: the new era did not produce a new man.

The term *Homo Sovieticus* therefore was first of all the product of political struggle against communism undertaken by intellectuals from Eastern Europe and the Soviet Union. Having experienced and understood the system, these individuals were able to share their critical observations about how the system operated and how it impacted peoples' mentality and behaviour. In their critical comments about *Homo Sovieticus*, they criticized the regime. In some ways, the work of these intellectuals who took an anti-regime stance, followed the traditions of *intelligentsia* in pre-tsarist Russia. Seeing the main role of intellectuals to be a moral and a critical voice vis-à-vis the authorities and institutions has been one of the mainstays in Russian and Eastern European debates about intellectuals and their social identity.[10]

Today this term, along with its Cold War-era connotations, coexists with other meanings created in Russia about what it means to be Soviet and what it means to be Russian. After the collapse of communism different conceptualizations were developed. The new context opened spaces for the analysis that differed from the dominant understandings associated with the Cold War. In academia and especially in the human sciences of history, anthropology and cultural studies, these new ideas and approaches promoted by new generations of scholars who developed revisionist and post-revisionist accounts of Soviet society and politics. The public sphere, however, especially after the 2014 Crimea annexation, experienced a throwback to older, more negative meanings. The idea of *Homo Sovieticus* understood as encompassing everything that was wrong with and in the Soviet Union proved hard to die out. Today it is linked to Putin's regime and is animated by fears of authoritarian and revanchist Russia.

I end the book with a brief look at pre-war Russian society and the trendsetters and opinion leaders inspiring the Russian youth before the Russian army invaded Ukraine on February 24, 2022. The survey of some of these recent ideas, norms and meanings that seem to have resonated in the Russian society suggests the contours of *Homo post-sovieticus*. I personally like to think and hope that these new ideas and meanings are the future of Russia. But without understanding the origins of the past ideas and meanings, we run the danger of entrapping ourselves in them. Awareness, psychologists argue, is the first step in the process of change. While the change would have to come from within Russia, the outside world would have to give that change a chance. It starts at the level of ideas.

CHAPTER 2
HOMO SOVIETICUS AS EASTERN EUROPEAN DISSENT

Politics is a treacherous business. It often divides the world into two. One side is right and the other is wrong. As the German philosopher Carl Schmidt (1888–1985) suggested, the concept of the political could be reduced to the existential distinction between a friend and an enemy. This definition of the political certainly applied in the era of the Cold War.

Despite the collective anti-Nazi effort during the war that brought the Soviets, Americans, British and French together, Europe became divided almost immediately after the end of the war. Winston Churchill's famous 1946 Fulton speech became the first public declaration of this divide: 'From Stettin in the Baltic to Trieste in the Adriatic, an iron curtain has descended across the Continent'. These words took a material form a few years later, in 1961, when the GDR authorities erected a concrete wall separating the Soviet-controlled part of the city from West Berlin. This measure sought to contain an increasing emigration from the Soviet-controlled part of the city into the West.

The relations between the United States and the Soviet Union defined the ups and downs of the Cold War. The dangerous confrontation between these two countries over the stationing of nuclear missiles in Cuba in 1962 became one of the tensest moments in the post-war era, when the Cold War could have turned hot. The détente of the 1970s, on the other hand, brought an easing of geopolitical tensions between the two countries. Joint space programmes and the historical handshake in space between a Soviet cosmonaut Alexei Leonov and an American Brigadier General

Thomas Stafford in 1975 became an important symbolic moment in Cold War history demonstrating that the two superpowers could work together on joint missions. The détente ended in 1979 with the Soviet invasion of Afghanistan. Mikhail Gorbachev launched his perestroika six years later, in 1985.

Domestically, life in the Soviet Union evolved after the Second World War, allowing observers to differentiate between periods roughly corresponding to decades. Khrushchev's destalinization campaign that started with the Secret Speech in 1956 brought about the cultural and political thaw of the late 1950s and early 1960s, a period of eased censorship taking its name from Ilya Ehrenburg's 1954 novel *The Thaw*. This brief period unleashed creative energies in the cultural sphere and the more generalized optimistic belief in the future – symbolized among other things by the achievements in Soviet space exploration and the Soviet success in sending the first human to space. The late Soviet non-conformist art (also known as counterculture) emerged during these years as well. It was driven underground after the infamous encounter the Soviet leader, Nikita Khrushchev, had at the Moscow Manege exhibition in 1962 when he described the avant-garde works as 'dogshit'.

The active search for new forms and meanings in painting, poetry and arts brought into being numerous 'deterritorialized milieus' in which the Soviet people lived and created (Yurchak 2013). The term 'internal emigration' captures well the creative practices of carving out the spaces that allowed for new forms, relations and meaning to emerge in the decades following a brief liberalization of the Thaw period. These new spaces – shared by small groups of individuals who could access them – co-existed with the official, state-controlled public sphere. Different Soviet writers – Sergei Dovlatov, Vasily Aksenov, Vladimir Bukovsky – described these practices of withdrawal from the system into the internal chambers of one's own spirit.[1] Such internal 'exile' co-existed with growing defections and emigration from the Soviet Union, especially during the 1970s, when many Soviet Jews were allowed to leave the country. The cases of defection from the Soviet Union as well as books and other banned, dissident writings smuggled from the country revealed a gap between the official public pronouncements of the Soviet government and the real social and political challenges in the country.

Before Soviet defections to the West, came the political émigrés from Eastern European countries where communism was imposed after the war. Their anti-regime ideas received much acclaim in the West and became the main pre-cursors to *Homo Sovieticus*.

On the edge between poetry and politics

Czeslaw Miłosz, a beloved Polish writer and a poet who would receive a Nobel Prize for literature in 1980, is better known in the West for his prose work. His non-fiction book titled *The Captive Mind* (1953) was the first incisive analysis of the variety of psychological and cultural props at work in making intellectuals surrender to the communist ideology and accept new authority and life that does not allow for freedom of thought and creation. Countering the simplistic and familiar juxtapositions between free-minded intellectuals and a despotic regime, Miłosz looked into the processes of ideological and institutional seduction taking hold over cultural elites in a specific historical context of Poland coming out of the destruction associated with the Second World War. In his creative work of poetry Miłosz made an effort to move away from political analysis into the metaphysical realm. He criticized even his benevolent reviewers for recognizing his work for the wrong reasons. He believed, 'The voice of a poet should be purer and more distinct than the noise (or confused music) of History'.[2] Nonetheless, his *The Captive Mind* is still read and discussed as a piercing analysis of the lure of ideas that led people away from freedom.

Miłosz was born in 1911 in Lithuania, to a Polish noble family. He studied in Vilno (now Vilnius) and Paris and, by the 1930s, gained a reputation as a leading figure in Polish poetry. He spent the war years in occupied Warsaw helping the underground resistance movement with publications. The end of war did not bring Poland its sovereignty. At the Yalta conference in February 1945 Stalin demanded that a pro-communist government would be formed in Poland forcing Churchill and Roosevelt to agree. Freed from the Nazis, the country fell under Soviet control and went through the process of Sovietization involving collectivization of land, nationalization of industries and the transformation of political institutions in accord with the Soviet state.

The extent of these drastic changes was not evident from the outset. Miłosz supported socialist ideas and was initially predisposed positively to the post-war regime in Poland hoping the new system will bring social justice. Recognized for his underground work, Miłosz joined the diplomatic corps even though he did not join the Communist Party. He was sent to the Polish Embassy in Washington, DC, as a cultural attaché responsible for promoting Polish culture in the United States at the time when the United States itself was turning increasingly and virulently anti-communist.

In those first post-war years Miłosz faced an acute inner conflict. He was at once a representative of a communist regime and a talented poet. He felt patriotic loyalty to Polish culture and literature but he also had a desire for artistic freedom increasingly encroached upon by the system established in his country. He expressed some of these struggles in his 1948 poem 'Treatise on Morals', questioning the moral cost of the new political system. The historical determinism proclaimed by Marxist ideology led to the negation of individual responsibility as Miłosz understood it (Franaszek 2011). This controversial poem did not follow the expected ideological line and was received with public silence. It gained prominence only later, in the 1980s, among the non-conformist Polish intellectuals (Mazurska 2013: 70).

With the growing Stalinization in Poland after 1948, Miłosz lost trust with the Polish authorities. He was recalled from Washington in 1950 and assigned to a new post in Paris. Earlier, during his 1949 trip to Warsaw, the writer experienced a sense of shock with the extent of material and spiritual deprivation that engulfed the Polish society after the war. He generalized his impressions from that trip in *The Captive Mind* as follows:

In the countries of the New Faith the cities lose their former aspect. The liquidation of small private enterprises gives the streets a stiff and institutional look. The chronic lack of consumer goods renders the crowds uniformly gray and uniformly indigent. When consumer products do appear, they are of a single second-rate quality. [Fear paralyzes individuality and makes people adjust themselves as much as possible to the average type in their gestures, clothing, and facial expressions.] The new buildings are monumental and oppressive, lightness and charm in architecture being condemned as formalistic. (66)

The massive changes associated with the growing state control and repression against the political opponents were unmistakably clear. The growing ideological and institutional pressure to conform to the newly instituted, rigid set of ideas essentially imposed from Moscow affected the Polish cultural elite first of all. Following the Soviet cultural model and propaganda mechanisms, the communist government saw a great promise in employing literary and artistic creativity for promoting a socialist worldview. Following the official introduction of social realism to the Polish literature and arts the more liberal publishing policy was replaced by the 'production plan' in literature (Mazurska 2013: 74). Fulfilling the plan meant writing prose and poetry on such ideologically correct themes as class struggle, workers' life, Polish-Soviet friendship and panegyrics to the Soviet leader Joseph Stalin.

Troubled with the totalitarian direction his country has taken and the moral compromises writers and intellectuals were compelled to make, Miłosz decided to leave. The decision was made in the conditions of a personal crisis. The writer found himself unable to write poems and unwilling to conform to the expectations imposed by the system (Mazurska 2013: 85). Feeling imprisoned in Paris, the writer returned to Warsaw to try to improve his situation but, instead, had his passport taken away from him. Only the help of his friends helped him to escape 'the deadly embrace of his socialist homeland' (Mazurska 2013: 93). Polish Minister of Foreign Affairs had to convince the president of Poland, Bolesław Bierut, to let Miłosz leave the country. The writer was granted asylum in France in February 1951.

Europe was in the midst of the Cold War. The political and ideological clash between the United States and the Soviet Union was played out in the sphere of arts and literature as well. A political émigré in Paris, Miłosz was quickly integrated into the cultural front of this war. Paris was the headquarters of the Congress for Cultural Freedom (CCF) – a transatlantic initiative founded in 1950 in West Berlin to bring together and support leftist intellectuals opposed to Stalinism and fascism. Such world-renowned intellectuals as Julian Huxley, Arthur Koestler, Arthur Schlesinger Jr., Sidney Hook, Carl Jaspers, Tennessee Williams and many others sought to counter Soviet propaganda and advance the ideas of freedom and human dignity (it was revealed in 1967 that the CCF activities were supported and funded by the CIA). It is at the CCF meetings in 1951 that Miłosz, who immediately became a celebrity in these Western circles, shared his insights about the practice of intellectual life under communism, offering a 'key to the mind of those seduced by Marxism and communism' (Mazurska 2013: 103–4). His ideas were in high demand. Many of these left-leaning intellectuals in CCF had their own history of infatuation with the Soviet system.

The intellectual impetus associated with the CCF and Miłosz's engagement in seminars and discussions in Paris resulted in his first book, *The Captive Mind*, published in exile in 1953.

It incorporated the writer's insights about the different paths of intellectual adaptation to and even attraction to the system and the new ideology, labelled in the book as the New Faith. As an intellectual who himself lived through the seduction by Marxism and the communist regime, facing the moral ambiguities and compromises expected on the way, the book represented a partly autobiographical and reflexive exercise written not only for the public, but as a way to 'exorcise' the writer's own ideological fascination with and illusions created by the New Faith. For Miłosz's, the book was 'a battlefield, in which I have given shape to my combat with the doctrine I have rejected' (*The Captive Mind*, XIII).

The Captive Mind examines the lives of four prototypes: Alpha, Beta, Gamma and Delta. Each of these characters was hiding real people – Polish writers Miłosz knew well. Each of them provided an example of different aspects and mechanisms of seduction by the New Faith.

The first one dealt with the ideological appeal of Marxist ideology in the period of *ideological vacuum and thirst for new ideas*. Miłosz himself was attracted to leftist ideas, rejecting the right-wing nationalism and believing, along with many of his friends, that the agrarian social structure of the interwar Poland needed to be changed. This search for new ideas was real, even in the West, where social critique of capitalist consumerism and individual alienation was widespread among the intellectuals and youth during the 1930s. Many notable leftists in the United States and Europe turned to the Soviet Union as an example of a different path and the Soviet government skillfully used them to promote its sociopolitical model (David-Fox 2011).

Besides this thirst for new ideas, some features specific to Marxism played a role too. The idea of *historical determinism* deeply engrained in Marxist ideology was another source of intellectual appeal. The notion of historical determinism added a sense of inevitability to the unfolding 'logic of history' freeing individuals of their moral responsibility for any evils committed for the sake of these ideas. Miłosz felt that the New Faith crippled critical reasoning. Any negative outcomes associated with the system could be viewed as inevitable steps on the path of the historical progress.

The desire of Polish intellectuals to be integrated into society, and *overcome the traditional alienation* from the masses represented another important reason that made Marxism appealing to intellectuals (Mazurska 2013: 122). This is another commonality in the history of many Eastern European countries. The Russian revolutionary tradition includes an entire reformist movement – *narodnichestvo* ('going to the people') – of the second half of the nineteenth century, that involved a short period of time when Russian intellectuals having become aware of their responsibility to the 'people' saw it as their mission to educate the peasants. Staying in touch with land and peasant traditions was important in post-war Poland too. Paweł Pawlikowski's 2018 film *Cold War* – set out as a story of a musician travelling through Polish countryside, presumably on the orders of the communist government, to collect and preserve the old tunes – is a good case demonstrating these concerns.

The last mechanism of seduction encompassed a common *human desire for recognition*, fame and prestige. The Soviet-style communist system in Poland had reserved a very important space for intellectuals and cultural elites seen to be essential for promoting socialism and advancing the goals of the system in the masses. Poetry and literature were seen as a forum for political propaganda and the young writers who subjected themselves to the norms of social realism were showered with financial and administrative support, institutional recognition and guaranteed publications. Those who did not – found themselves in the internal or external exile, at best. Miłosz himself shared later on: 'They wanted to make me someone who is feted with laurels and applause in public, and it is only backstage that they punch him in the face'.[3]

Miłosz's nuanced analysis in *The Captive Mind* highlighted the various socio-psychological drivers that came together in a post-war Polish society to shape the ideological choices made by the cultural elites. Ideas matter and their influence depends on the 'right place and the right time'. Unlike many anti-communist writings that presented the post-war context in black-and-white terms focusing on repression on one side and freedom on the other, Miłosz depicted a more complex reality. This reality contained different elements that prepared the ground for accepting the New Faith: the ideological vacuum and a search for new ideas, Marxist analytical strength, pre-existing aspirations of the Polish intellectual class and last, but not least, simple human psychology that applies across time and space. Miłosz was also very upfront that he wrote *The Captive Mind* for the Western audience, as an attempt to explain the psychological processes at work not only in Poland, but in other countries that have encountered the New Faith.

Besides the writer's stories in the first part of the book, Miłosz provided an insightful discussion of the system's expectations for developing a new man:

'The development of a new man' is the key point in the New Faith's program.

The 'new man' is conditioned to acknowledge the good of the whole as the sole norm of his behavior. He thinks and reacts like others; is modest, industrious, satisfied with what the state gives him; limits his private life to nights spent at home and passes all the rest of his time amidst his companions at work or at play, observing them carefully and reporting their actions and opinions to the authorities. Informing was and is known in many civilizations, but the New Faith declares it a cardinal virtue of the good citizen. (76)

If biting dogs can be divided into two main categories, noisy and brutal, or silent and slyly vicious, then the second variety would seem most privileged in the countries of the New Faith. Forty or fifty years of education in these new ethical maxims must create a new and irretrievable species of mankind. The 'new man' is not merely a postulate. He is beginning to become a reality. (77)

The Captive Mind won Miłosz widespread popularity and prominence in the West. While it interrogated the behaviour and attitudes of cultural elites under communism, its ideas were generalized for the masses and the book title captured the more general tendencies of life under communism. It was translated into many languages (not surprisingly, it was banned in Poland) and turned into one of the classic works on totalitarianism, frequently compared to Orwell's *1984*. It was Miłosz's main political essay recognized in the West but the writer continued his creative work outside politics, staying on the path of continued self-reflection and searching. In his poetry he transcended politics and moralizing, focusing more on universal questions of the human condition.[4] He published an autobiographical novel, *The Issa Valley*, in 1955 and another self-exploratory memoir, *Native Realm: A Search for Self-Definition* appeared in 1959. *Native Realm* was later viewed as the work that developed an antidote to the psychological forces the author described in *The Captive Mind* (Fanailova 2011). The only answer to the attraction of the certainty of faith and the brilliant logic of historical inevitability Miłosz saw in the humble love and appreciation for local expressions of life and humanity, in all their possible imperfections. Marxism yielded to humanism.

In 1960 Miłosz moved to Berkeley, California, where he quickly advanced to become professor at the Department of Slavic Languages and Literatures. He received a Nobel Prize for his literary work in

1980 and lived to see political transformation in his native Lithuania and Poland. His concept of the captive mind that ensnared the peoples of his homeland remained incredibly influential.

A flight from the unbearable

Other Eastern European countries had their own Orwells. Georgy Markov (1929–78), a Bulgarian writer, belonged to the category of young talented writers who joined the literary field in Bulgaria at the moment of Khruschev's thaw. Coming from a family of a military serviceman and a housewife, Markov was unlike most of his peer intellectuals and writers. He studied to be a chemical engineer and started out working in a factory. Markov turned to writing after he fell ill with tuberculosis and was confined in the hospital for lengthy periods of time. His quick literary success with first short stories was consolidated after he received a national award and a membership in Bulgarian Writers' Union for his third novel, *Men*, published in 1962. He continued to publish other novels and started a career of a playwright in 1963, entering theatre circles as well. The new institutional affiliation and national recognition afforded Markov a lifestyle of material benefits and prestige. The new cultural elite was seen to be vital for raising patriotic citizens and therefore highly valued by the government. As part of that elite, Markov could now enjoy partying and mingling with the Communist Party members. He was one of the few writers who attended private gatherings organized by Todor Zhivkov, the General Secretary of the Communist Party of Bulgaria. Later, in his memoirs Markov wrote: 'I passed from the world of the ordinary Bulgarian citizen deprived of his basic rights into the world of those who had "set up a state for themselves".'[5]

These privileges and luxurious lifestyle could only be enjoyed, of course, if one played along and toed the party line. Balancing on the edge of the acceptable, Markov realized that the moral compromises required of him in this system were hard to endure. It worked for a while as the writer expanded into theatre, where he could try to avoid the ideologically and stylistically restrictive socialist realism. Markov's plays turned into the 'exilic shelter' for a disillusioned writer who relied increasingly on Aesopian language and dark pessimism.[6] Yet the broader political environment in the country turned more restrictive and Markov confronted an increasing censorship of his work in the second half of the 1960s. His novels were not printed and many of his plays were never staged or removed from the repertoire of theatres by the censors. One of Markov's novels, *The Great Roof*, was written after the real disaster of a fallen roof of the steel factory that killed workers. This story turned into a metaphor for the unfulfilled promises of Bulgarian socialism. The publication of the novel was halted when at the printing press.

The tension around Markov increased dramatically after the premier of his play *I Was Him* (*Ya byl im*) on 15 June 1969 attended by a general audience as well as the party officials. This was a controversial political satire written in the aftermath of Prague Spring in Czechoslovakia. In this work Markov drew a grotesque picture of nepotism, slavishness and incompetence using the example of the career path of an engineer in a machine factory mistaken for a nephew of a big minister. On the day of a premier, Markov was presumably tipped by a friend in the top establishment about impending danger and decided to leave Bulgaria to avoid potential arrest. Without any friends and resources, he first passed through Italy, where his émigré brother lived, and later settled in London.

Markov did not burn the bridges to Bulgaria immediately. Although he was fired from his editorial position in a state-owned publishing house, some of his personal letters reveal a state of undecidedness about the future. But back home rumours spread about his defection, and renewing his international passport proved to be difficult.[7] In the fall of 1970 Markov asked for a political asylum in Great Britain.

Markov's intimate knowledge of the communist regime and his critical stance towards the system were in demand in the West in the midst of the Cold War. Quickly learning English, he found a job in the Bulgarian section of the BBC. Besides his work there, he also freelanced for Radio Free Europe (RFE) and the German Deutsche Welle, where he contributed his cultural and political writings on

Bulgaria. His weekly radio broadcasts for the US-sponsored RFE, *In Absentia Reports about Bulgaria*, incorporated short essays about his life in communist Bulgaria. These reports reached not only the Western audience but also the growing numbers of his Bulgarian compatriots who could tune into the short wavelengths. The Bulgarian audience loved Markov's reports: they were personal and candid.

From his formerly privileged position Markov was able to expose the secret lives of high-ranking officials, intellectuals and writers, and share his experiences with the more common folks from the margins of the society.

In his *The Captive Mind* Miłosz wrote about party admission in the following way:

> Demands made upon Party members are exceedingly harsh . . . admission to the Party is not unlike entrance into a religious order; and the literature of the New Faith treats this act with a gravity equal to that with which Catholic literature speaks of the vows of young nuns. (75)

These observations applied in Bulgaria, too. The exposure of cynicism, careerism and nepotism among the communist officials who were expected to be the 'brahmins' of the system became a subversive tool in Markov's hands. His narratives showed a big gap between the official claims, promises and the reality of lived socialism. Following the strategy of other dissidents in the Soviet bloc, Markov critiqued the regime from the position of the communist ideal. This made his critique much more powerful and resonant among his compatriots who were brought up with such ideals in mind. There were in total 137 broadcasts of these *In Absentia Reports* aired between November 1975 and June 1978.

In the last of these reports, Markov shared his sense of the reasons for his exile. In an essay titled *The Feeling of Unbearableness* (*Chuvstvo nevynosimosti*), he first recounted the unbearable pain of not being able to say the last goodbye to his dying father because the communist authorities could not forgive the writer who defected to the West.

Markov also described this sense of unbearableness as a regular part of life in communist Bulgaria:

> I felt that I could not tolerate anymore the atmosphere in which I lived, my work, and my relationships. [...] I realized that over many years I have not really experienced any joy because everything was poisoned by this sense of unbearableness. If you had a certain sense of yourself and thought you were something and then noticed how you are gradually but inevitably becoming something else, then probably you will face a moment when you would want to destroy the mirror or your head. From the ethical perspective, there was a sense of double ignobility – towards others and towards one's own self. Beyond any ethical categories, this was a sense of hopelessness.

Markov used these words to describe his state of mind at the moment of his departure – when he was circling Sofia one last time – before his departure from Bulgaria. It is the psychological state of a person who made a pragmatic decision to leave facing a threat of political repression. As such, through these thoughts Markov was trying to come to terms with the decision that ended his life as he knew it. He was abandoning his land, his culture, his people and his parents, fully aware that he was unlikely to be able to return.

Meanwhile, already in the first year of Markov's work for BBC and Deutsche Welle, the Bulgarian authorities launched a political campaign against him that culminated in a political trial in 1972. After a two-week trial the writer was sentenced in absentia to six years and six months in prison for anti-communist propaganda.

The stability and legitimacy of communist regimes rested on a comprehensive information control and intense cultural and ideological indoctrination of the population. Communist governments persecuted *dissent* (*inakomyslie*) and from the governments' perspective such radio broadcasts represented an *ideological sabotage* and a criminal offence. Therefore, for the Bulgarian government and intelligence services Markov turned into a continuing annoyance and a political threat. Markov's earlier, close friendship to Todor Zhivkov's daughter Lyudmila and his unsightly depiction of Bulgaria's political leader added an element of personal vendetta in the relationship of the writer and Bulgaria's communist leader. His immigrant activities were followed closely by the intelligence services that viewed him as a traitor and issued death threats. They followed up their threats with the request for the KGB's help in taking care of this problem.

On 8 September 1978, while walking on the Waterloo bridge in London, Markov was poisoned with a ricin-tipped umbrella by Bulgarian secret services with likely logistical support from the KGB. He died in the hospital few days after the poisoning. He was forty-nine.

After the collapse of communism, Markov's name turned into a symbol of Bulgarian anti-communism. His assassination – the infamous 'umbrella affair' – symbolized the horrors of the Soviet-style totalitarianism unforgiving of the former citizens who cross to the other side. Experiencing a second rise to fame Markov was referred to as the 'Bulgarian Orwell' and was awarded posthumously in 2000 the Order of Stara Planina, the country's most prestigious state honour (Karkov 2018: 156).

More nuanced interpretations of Markov's work steer away from a black-and-white picture that emerged after his death of a person who chose the free world over the one enslaved by the totalitarian system and who was anti-communist at heart. Reviewing his intellectual heritage Nikolay Karkov argues that 'at the heart of Markov's work there is also a grand communist vision, and Idea of communism, which significantly tempers and qualifies his critique of state socialism' (Karkov 2018: 166). While critical of the state socialism, a 'life under the lid' was still 'more alive, more resonant, more colorful' for Markov (Karkov 2018: 157). Markov himself rejected the black-and-white pictures preferred in the West. In a letter to another exiled writer Markov wrote:

I hope you share my disillusionment for ever being understood by our western readers. Their perception [of the East] is, at best, childish and naive, and, at worse, cynical . . . The West accepted enthusiastically the picture of the East which Solzhenitsyn painted, because it is emotional and simple like a 'horror movie' whereas the reality [there] is far more complex and not that exotic.[8]

In his stories and reports about life in Bulgaria Markov developed ideas that, on the one hand, resonated with Marxist analysis of 'commodity fetishism' and 'social alienation' and, on the other hand, provided a post-colonial reading of popular 'self-marginalization' expressed in Bulgarian obsession with Western things: objects, people and culture. Markov developed a criticism of the 'petty bourgeois mentality' developing in Bulgaria with the wave of consumerism spreading after the relative softening in the post-Stalinist era and the emergence of new mechanisms of social control that relied, in the Bulgarian context, on the promotion of tourism and raising the general well-being of the Bulgarian citizens (Karkov 2018: 159). These observations might fit even better the realities unfolding after the collapse of communism, as the country went through privatization and economic and political reforms.

Neither Miłosz nor Markov fit neatly the binary framework of the Cold War that divided the world into two opposite camps with one representing the evil and the other, the paradise on Earth. They are frequently placed on one side of this struggle – as critics of totalitarianism. After all, their analysis of life under communism presaged the concept of *Homo Sovieticus* and is an important part of the literature on totalitarian systems. But neither of them idealized the West and both of them developed critical reflections about their lives in the West as well, looking for a 'third way'. The product of their times and surroundings, they took an anti-regime stance but also, in their own ways, and particularly in the case of Cheslaw Miłosz, they tried to transcend the politics of their times. Both writers need to be accorded a more nuanced interpretation than they are usually allowed.

Conclusion

Communism encouraged and thrived on conformity and individual adaptation to systemic pressures and rules. Individual effort was recognized only if it went along with the 'party line' and was intended to promote the goals of the state. The Communist Party-state developed its own rules for career advancement and those who accepted the system's inevitability (i.e. the majority), played by rules imposed from above. Those who refused to adjust, those who rejected the necessity of bending their thinking and expression to accord to the ideological demands, those who had reasons to doubt and the strength to resist, confronted the system. Different forms of dissent proliferated in the Soviet Union and other countries of the socialist bloc in the post-Stalinist period. Disseminating alternative information (expressed in the circulation of *samizdat* in the Soviet Union), writing critical reviews and programmatic statements and more particularized protests against political repression became one of the predominant ways of such intellectual resistance.

Some dissenters emigrated to the West. Their escapes were a testament to their recognition, privileged status and connections they had inside and outside their countries. Many others, who wanted to cross the communist state boundaries, could not. But it was also a matter of their moral choice. The escape to the West of the most talented writers, poets and artists amounted to 'committing suicide', at least in terms of their creativity. Abandoning the lands that inspired them, the language they spoke and created in and the audiences for whom they wrote – at the time when any return was inconceivable – could only be done in despair. The emigration meant there is no looking back, there is no return. It took a lot of courage.

The dissenters who were able to escape turned into an important source of information for the Western public about life under communism. Their observations about the ways communism leaves its mental imprints in an individual were foundational for the development of the term *Homo Sovieticus*. The new distance from the communist environment and the welcome embrace in the West ensured these ideas were published and widely discussed. They were quite consistent with the analytical discussions about totalitarianism emerging at that time in the social sciences. As the world divided into two, so did the understanding of human subjectivity. The free capitalist West was seen to allow for the emergence of an idealized autonomous, liberal self, while the communist system brought into being *Homo Sovieticus*, the oppressed Soviet subject who lacked the autonomy, legal rights and protections and was brainwashed by totalitarian ideology (Krylova 2000).

CHAPTER 3
HOMO SOVIETICUS AS SOVIET DISSENT

Anti-Soviet and anti-communist dissent emerged not only in the countries of the socialist bloc that were forced on the path of communism after the Second World War. Within the Soviet Union as well, the politics of anti-Stalinism after the 1956 Secret Speech produced a political and cultural relaxation of the Thaw period that did not last very long. Brezhnev's leadership that began in 1964 took the country in a more conservative direction, favouring political stability above all other concerns. The second half of the 1960s in the Soviet Union saw the emergence of a dissident movement that placed human rights and freedom of conscience at the centre of the political agenda of those who disagreed with the policies and the moral foundations of the Soviet regime.

The image of ideological unity and perceived superiority of the Soviet system promoted by Soviet propaganda were among the essential foundations of the system's stability. The dissident activities that involved circulating and publishing information that the Soviet authorities kept secret undermined these foundations. The Soviet government took different measures to suppress dissidents. The early policy of sending them to labour camps was later supplemented by measures of forced hospitalization in psychiatric institutions, forced emigration and internal exile. In his recent memoir *The Dissidents* (2020: 147), Peter Reddaway, a British-American political scientist closely involved in helping the dissidents and disseminating their writings in the West, cites the following figures for political prosecutions in the Soviet Union provided by Yuri Andropov, the KGB head: 8,664 for 1959–66 and 4,879 for 1967–74. These numbers were kept relatively low by 'prophylaxis' – preventive talks and warnings issued by the KGB agents – that amounted, according to Andropov's report, to 121,406 cases.

As with Eastern European intellectuals opposing the system, Soviet dissidents (also referred to as *inakomysliashchie*) developed in writing their views about how the system impacted an individual. This chapter zooms in on the ideas of two well-known Soviet intellectuals, who contributed to the negative connotation of *Homo Sovieticus* linking it to the concept of totalitarianism and systemic oppression.

On the life and ideas of a communist contrarian

Alexander Zinoviev is often credited with coining the term *Homo Sovieticus* that he used as the title of his 1981 book. A passionate and determined contrarian all his life, he was born as a sixth child to a peasant family from the Kostroma region in 1922. Zinoviev always defied social conformity and went against the dominant views at the time of the most brutal Stalinism, the anti-Stalinist Khrushchev era, the Brezhnev era, during his life in Germany and, finally, in post-Soviet Russia. Coming a full circle, in the last years of his life in new Russia, Zinoviev turned into an apologist of the Soviet Union. Perhaps due to this fact and Zinoviev's late anti-Westernism, in October 2021 Russia's president signed a decree about the national celebration of Zinoviev's 100-year anniversary.[1]

Zinoviev's family moved to Moscow a few years after Sasha was born and the talented boy was able to study in a more advanced Moscow school. They lived in a small room in a communal apartment. Early on Sasha had to toughen up to survive the Moscow street-life that involved fights and rough tests for the newcomers who have not yet established their positions in the street 'gopnik' hierarchy.

Zinoviev was a bright student and after school graduation with the highest honours, he was admitted in 1939 to the elite Moscow Institute of Philosophy, Literature and History (*MIFLI*). During his student years in the late 1930s Zinoviev developed his anti-Stalinist views that interfered with his career plans. With his rural origins, Zinoviev knew very well the sorry fate of the villages and kolkhozes after the forced Soviet collectivization of the early thirties. He tells the story in his autobiographical *The Flight of Our Youth (Nashey Iunosti Polet)* how in 1939, at his institute seminar, he shared his sharp criticism and his understanding of the situation in the countryside. As normally happened in those times, such public vocalization of a negative stance towards the government policy drew a 'necessary reaction' on the part of the 'responsible organs'. Zinoviev was pressured by Komsomol officials and institute officials to abandon his views and admit to his 'grave' mistakes. Not yielding to pressure, he was dismissed from both.

Even before that incident, Alexander got involved in a small conspiratorial circle that deliberated on whether or not to murder Stalin. After that seminar Zinoviev, a young man, seventeen years old, came under the radar of NKVD (People's Commissariat for Internal Affairs), the notorious Soviet secret police. Zinoviev literally ran away as he was escorted back from a conversation in the Lubyanka, their HQ. He left his apartment, took a train away from Moscow and found himself about 100 km away. He was apprehended six months later and joined the army at a time when the Soviet Union was attacked by Nazi Germany in June 1941. During the war he first served in a tank unit and later learned to fly, earning medals for heroism for his missions. After the war he earned his graduate and post-graduate degrees from Moscow State University and then stayed to teach at the university and work for the Academy of Science on mathematical logic and the methodology of science.

Going against the system during the Khrushchev era and later, during the Brezhnev era, by 1974 Zinoviev was deeply isolated. It was his first book, *The Yawning Heights*, a sharp satire on life in the Soviet Union published in Switzerland in 1976, that led the authorities to fire Zinoviev from his jobs, expel from the Communist Party and strip him of his honours and medals. This book was an outburst of his pent-up thoughts and feelings about the system he lived in. Written in a very brief period (during 1975), this biting commentary on Soviet realities had an effect of an explosion on those who read it. While illegal in the Soviet Union, it was circulated through the informal networks of samizdat and was often read within a matter of one to two nights.[2] Eclectic in style, it combined prose and poetry with a pseudo-scientific style, vulgarisms and a rough humour. While the characters in the novel were all invented, some of them had clear allusions to real Soviet leaders, including Stalin and Khruschev.

Later, in 1978 Zinoviev published another anti-communist and anti-Soviet novel *The Radiant Future*, which again, in a satirical format familiar from his earlier novel, exposed the huge gap between the empty promises and slogans of the communist system and the uninspiring, boring reality that surrounded everyone. The book title borrowed from one of those publicly displayed communist slogans: 'Long Live Communism – the Radiant Future of All Mankind'. *The Radiant Future* contained personal insults about Leonid Brezhnev, the General Secretary of the Communist Party of the Soviet Union (CPSU). After weighing various options (including the one when the author would be sent to a psychiatric hospital), the authorities allowed Zinoviev to emigrate to Germany. Zinoviev already had a job invitation from Germany and a high-ranking lobbying on his behalf from the Western leaders. Zinoviev's incarceration would have likely produced a wave of anti-Soviet media coverage in the West.

Zinoviev remained a prolific writer and a darling of the Western media after his departure from the Soviet Union. In Germany, while teaching at the University of Munich, Zinoviev wrote other sociological novels critical of the Soviet Union, including his *The Reality of Communism* (1984) and *Homo Sovieticus* (1981). All his writings of the 1970s–1980s could be compared to Georgy Markov's earlier plays and novels written in Bulgaria that portrayed the crude realities of life under communism differing sharply with the official promises and declarations of the communist government. In Zinoviev's case, there was an additional coarseness and intentional, conspicuous offensiveness and harshness in his writing that made publishing his work in the Soviet Union unimaginable. His stylistic eclecticism and innovation reflected in the kaleidoscopic format of his writing combining dialogues, internal monologues with parody and verse also added uniqueness to his creative talents and literary force.

True to his contrarian character and unlike many émigrés of that era, Zinoviev never joined dissident circles in the West. One might have expected, based on his anti-communist writings, that he would support Gorbachev's reforms. But Zinoviev never supported perestroika (coining a new term for it, '*katastroika*' in a different book) and took the Soviet collapse as a big tragedy. In a 1990 exchange with Boris Yeltsin on a French TV channel, Zinoviev confronted Yeltsin suggesting that the West wants the Soviet Union destroyed and that 'Gorbachev and Yeltsin get a pat on the back because the West thinks they are destroying the country'.[3]

By the early 1990s he turned his critical attention to the West, standing against its idealization held by so many Soviet (or former Soviet) citizens. In his 1997 dystopia, *Global Humant Hill (Globalny cheloveinik)*, Zinoviev depicted the Western social organization in ways that resemble his view of the Soviet society in *The Yawning Heights*. In both societies individual control is established through lies and propaganda. To the extent that the members of the society believe that they live in the best possible state, they do not realize their lack of freedom and do not protest. In his disillusionment with the West, Zinoviev repeated the painful experiences of other communist dissidents such as Miłosc and Markov discussed earlier. Aleksandr Solzhenitsyn – another famous Soviet dissident – also experienced such dramatic disappointment after his emigration from the Soviet Union. In his 1978 speech at Harvard University's commencement, Solzhenitsyn delivered a scathing assessment of the moral bankruptcy, selfishness, complacency and spiritual failure of the Western society.[4]

Zinoviev returned to Russia with his family in 1999, following the NATO bombing of Belgrade (Yugoslavia) that he criticized sharply. In his last years he taught again at Moscow State University, and led an active public life, continuing to write and advance the causes of individual resistance and freedom.

As evident from his life trajectory, Zinoviev was a rebel at heart. He started his intellectual path as an anti-Stalinist and commented on the origins of his anti-Stalinism as follows:

> My anti-Stalinism originated in unbearable living conditions of people in my surrounding. My personal hatred of Stalin was really a personification of my protest against these conditions.

But early on I started to think about the reasons of this monstrous (in my view) injustice. Towards the end of my schooling I was sure that the source of evil is in socialism (communism) itself. My personal hatred of Stalin gave way to an intellectual curiosity and a desire to understand the covert mechanisms of the socialist society that give rise to all the negative phenomena I witnessed so much. [. . .] Stalinism gradually turned for me from personal enemy into an object of research. (Nashei iunosti polet, 1983: 7)

Stalin's death brought an end to Zinoviev's anti-Stalinism. He described his personal 'existential' tragedy and compared himself to a 'repentant anti-Stalinist' he once met. (9)

In his 1983 autobiographical book about Stalinism, Zinoviev developed a full-scale defence of the system and the 'great epoch' that represented 'the only bright spot in the grey history of communism' (Zinoviev, 2010). Here Zinoviev provided numerous justifications to mass repressions of Stalin era citing their potential contribution to Soviet victory in the war, suggesting that people treated repressions as an adequate measure given the perceived sub-standard quality of the human material, noting that if Soviet citizens did not play active role in the denunciations, they feared they would be next, and so on. Zinoviev argued that many of Stalin's policy choices, such as the project of collectivization, were necessitated by history. Developing his vision of Stalin's leadership and Stalinism as a system Zinoviev saw Stalin as an embodiment of the Soviet nation who knew 'who we were and we knew that he knows' (Zinoviev, 2010). He admired cultural revolution in the Soviet Union as one of the greatest achievement of Stalinism (Zinoviev, 2010). The new society required new people – more educated and professionally fit. And Stalinism produced such an 'adequate society': 'a new man with a suitable social organization and a new social organization with the adequate man' (Zinoviev, 2010).

Many of Zinoviev's books and writings built off each other which sometimes brings up criticisms that after his path-breaking *The Yawning Heights* he was not able to write anything conceptually new.[5] The object of his attention did change, but his style and critical observations indeed repeated themselves. In 1981 Zinoviev wrote a book, *Homo Sovieticus*, dedicated specifically to the Soviet human material he was so critical of in many of his writings. He wrote it already when living in Germany, and it is clear from the introduction to the book that he responded in his writing to how the Soviet people were seen in the Western media.

While using the term *Homo Sovieticus* in the title, in the book Zinoviev abbreviates this term into *homosos* (or gomosos) – an offensive-sounding version of *Homo Sovieticus* that alludes, pejoratively, to a homosexual. Eliot Borenstein further transformed this term to *Homo sucker* noting that 'sos' is the Russian root for suck.[6] In the book's opening Zinoviev proclaims his desire to write a political novel about love between Russia and the West and he defines this love to be authentic and modern in that it is a homosexual type of love (Zinoviev, 2010). In the preface to his book Zinoviev presented his attitude towards *Homo Sovieticus* using a dialectical approach:

> This book is about a Soviet person as a new type of a human being. My relationship to that person is dual: love, respect and admiration for him stand side by side my hatred, contempt and dread for this person. I am homosos myself. Therefore, I will be cruel and merciless in my exposition.

Zinoviev admits not only the duality of his attitudes but also the numerous contradictions in his writing. The somewhat irrational style of writing is one of Zinoviev's signatures. In his book on Stalinism he himself refers to his words as irrational and defends his style by suggesting that human history is itself irrational and 'only human foolishness is rational' (*Nashei iunosti polet* p. 18). It is at times hard to believe that Zinoviev taught mathematical logic. His writing style often resembles a stream of consciousness driven by his conflicting views, emotions, nostalgia and youthful passions. Not surprising, he valued the dialectical approach so much. It allowed for the co-existence of contradictions. Contradictions were valued as a source of change.

The title of Zinoviev's *Homo Sovieticus* and its preface are a little misleading, however, because many human stories, conversations and incidents discussed in it actually concern Soviet immigrants in the West. Zinoviev's opening to the book also reveals that the author is reacting to Western debates about the soviet man and tries to 'out-do' the West in this endeavour. His recent position of an insider allows him to write a report (*otchet*) about *Homo Sovieticus* and he uses this format used in abundance in the Soviet Union. Just like with the relevant writings by Georgy Markov and Czeslaw Miłosz, discussed earlier, *Homo Sovieticus* is, to a large extent, an autobiographical work. The author himself is always in the centre of the story and all observations reflect Zinoviev's own personal experience and his personal outlook mediated by the context he found himself in and psychological challenges he faced in different stages of his life. In the book he recounts his experiences with the 'questioning' (допросы) he had to undergo (Western secret services, undoubtedly, were interested in anyone who left the Soviet Union at that time); his meetings with different types of people including the official authorities, intellectuals, other writers and Soviet émigrés; his unmet sexual needs; and a variety of other topics emerging from his life in emigration.

Most of his sociological novels, such as *Homo Sovieticus*, comprise a compilation of numerous short essays on various relevant subjects – hence the kaleidoscopic style of his writing. But there are some themes that get his repeated attention and not only in this book but also in others. The Soviet culture of collectivism is one such topic. For Zinoviev, collectivism was one of the achievements of the Stalinist era. He also linked collectivism to the Soviet leader. In his *Nashei iunosti polet*, Zinoviev wrote about collectivism in a very positive format:

After the revolution collectivism blossomed among millions of young souls that went through Soviet pre-war schooling. Stalin was a symbol and an embodiment of our sense of belonging to the whole, to brotherhood, to the united peoples' family. (21)

In *Homo Sovieticus*, Zinoviev writes about the value of collectives in personal lives of Soviet citizens and shares about his own personal experience of the loss of his collective due to emigration:

The detachment from the collective is biggest loss for the gomosos. I do not regret the loss of my friends and relatives, of my Moscow flat, of my good job. Every night and day I think about losing my collective. It is not necessarily my last laboratory or the institute that preceded the lab, but any type of collective. Being involved in the life of the collective is at the very basis of our psychology. The soul of gomosos is in his involvement in the life of the collective. (61)

Other features of *homosos* include (1) the lack of principled beliefs ('that's a feature of a Western person'); *homosos* has behavioral stereotypes instead; (2) the Soviet culture of denunciations that Zinoviev viewed as an element of 'peoples' power' and as a way the Soviet people participated in governance (p. 38); (3) the lack of sincerity (because it is silly to expect sincerity from *homosos* because he does not know how to be sincere even if he wanted it); (4) psychological plasticity, adaptiveness and lack of morals; (5) pro-government attitudes; (6) commitment to ideology, and so on. This list could be continued given Zinoviev's rich writing full of everyday observations and metaphors. What does emerge clearly from his writing is that he views *homosos* as a product of historical adaptation to the systemic pressures and institutional forces working in the Soviet Union. And in this understanding, Zinoviev is very close to Levada's conceptualization of the Soviet man, that would be discussed in the next chapter. Nonetheless, adhering to his dialectical vision, Zinoviev also viewed *homosos* as a contagious phenomenon that spreads to other regions. Also in a contradictory and deeply ironic fashion he ended his discussion by proclaiming that *homosos* is not a sign of degradation; rather, he is a super-human and a pinnacle of civilization: of course, of Soviet civilization (150).

Written in the early years of his émigré life in the West, this book conveys Zinoviev's growing nostalgia for his Soviet life. Comparing Western collectives to the Soviet ones, he complains Western collectives 'do not provide a sense of protection and a spiritual warmth that you get in Soviet collectives. The personal greedy interests are stronger and sharper here. People are colder and more ruthless' (62). The cynical and depreciating style he uses that could be considered an affront by anyone from East or West reading the book might hide the conflicted emotions all political émigrés are likely to experience and serve as a coping mechanism, too. In his later, autobiographical *Nashei iunosti polet*, Zinoviev shares openly about the Stalin era as the best period of his life that he would not trade for any other (Zinoviev, 2010).

Zinoviev's cynicism was not directed to *homosos* in particular. He was cynical about Westerners as well:

Do you think people in the West are more moral than us? I can count a large number of situations in which the western people look much worse than the homosos(y). For example, homosos(y) are much more empathetic towards their brothers. And they are not as greedy. However, homosos(y) are more considerate to others not because they are more moral but because of collectivism.

Zinoviev also shared his opinion on 'doublethinking' as a feature of *Homo Sovieticus*, commonly discussed by many observers then and now. The term 'doublethink' was coined by George Orwell in his book *1984* and referred to the individual ability to believe in contradictory ideas simultaneously. In more academic, psychological language 'doublethink' connotes the tolerance of cognitive inconsistency and is sometimes associated with or equated to hypocrisy:

There was no doublethinking. Doublethinking is a western invention done by people who do not understand the Soviet lifestyle and Soviet people. I am a communist not because I believe in Marxist fairy tales (few people believe in those in the Soviet Union), but because I was born, raised and educated in a communist society and I carry all the significant qualities of the Soviet man. What are these qualities? Well, for example, if you continue to ask me about my party membership, I would send you 'na . . .' They laughed. (45–6)

The last words in this quote represent a common Russian obscenity ('poslat na hui' translated as 'fuck off').

Most of Zinoviev's sociological novels are written as a compilation of long monologues, the many voices that develop different views and positions. His philosophy is not a systematically developed set of ideas but it is analytic in a sense that the author plays with analytical constructions and the dialectical logic that thrives on opposition, unpredictable conclusions and juxtapositions to the dominant views Zinoviev encountered in the Soviet Union as well as when he lived in the West. They are in many ways a reflection of the writer's contrarian, non-conformist character. He consistently took an original and oppositional stance to the ideas and trends that have dominated in any single moment in the places he lived. He admitted that himself: 'If someone would suggest things I do, I would have to oppose him', wrote Zinoviev in *Homo Sovieticus.*

Thus, while developing this, generally negative and detached, conception of *Homo Sovieticus,* Zinoviev also recognized the humanity of the 'Soviet person' who was not for him an immoral subject, but rather a human adaptation to the broader historical forces. Zinoviev's *homosos* was full of contradictions and emotions, and the portrait Zinoviev painted was very much shaped by his own embodied life experiences, historically situated in the period of the Cold War.

A defiant fight for freedom

Vladimir Bukovsky is another good example of the contrarian Soviet dissident whose love for freedom and opposition to the systemic pressures of the communist system defined his life, his activities and worldview. Bukovsky was born in 1942 in the Soviet town of Belebey in Bashkir Autonomous Soviet Socialist Republic (ASSR). His non-conformist attitudes and politically subversive behaviour surfaced early on in his life. He was thrown out of school for writing a satirical journal about Soviet life and was excluded from Moscow State University in 1961 for his political activities. It would not be an exaggeration to state that Bukovsky's entire adult life turned into a model of uncompromising, principled action dedicated to the cause of freedom and human rights in the Soviet Union. Between 1963 and

1971, Bukovsky survived four jail terms, and was twice incarcerated in psychiatric hospitals. He was freed from his last jail term in 1976, and exchanged for the leader of the Communist Party of Chile Luis Corvalan.[7] He probably would not have appreciated the comparison, but Vladimir Bukovsky was as committed to anti-communism as the early Bolsheviks were committed to revolution. The struggle against communism was Bukovsky's principal *raison d'etre*. Bukovsky writes in his memoirs that knowing he would get back into jail, he was driven by the desire to catch up on political action he missed while in jail, and to act even more intensely and purposefully, while he was free. Indeed, as many Bolsheviks dedicating their lives to their political cause, Bukovsky purposefully never married and had no children.

After the famous prisoner exchange in 1976 Bukovsky settled in the UK. His uncompromising fight against communism and the Soviet system continued abroad. He wrote political articles, engaged in campaigns, advised Western politicians and took a principled anti-statist, libertarian stance. In the West, he founded Resistance International, an organization that combined the dissidents who escaped the USSR. They organized public events to bring attention to issues of human rights abuses and lack of free speech in the Soviet Union.

Bukovsky did not believe in late Soviet perestroika policies and did not celebrate Gorbachev's reforms and leadership the way others in the West did. After the Soviet collapse, he returned to Russia and participated in the trial against the Communist Party in 1992. The trial by Russia's Constitutional Court exposed the crimes of the Soviet era but Boris Yeltsin wanted to avoid the witch-hunt against the rank-and-file Communists. Therefore, the trial did not turn into a Nuremberg for communism and did not lead to de-communization and lustration. The decision of the court to support Yeltsin's decree disbanding the CPSU and allow communists to form a new party, the Communist Party of the Russian Federation (CPRF), could be hailed as a victory by both sides. Based on his archival research in preparation for this trial, Bukovsky would later publish *Moskovsky protsess* (1996) translated into English later, as *Judgement in Moscow: Soviet Crimes and Western Complicity* (2019).

Bukovsky's view *of Homo Sovieticus* was intrinsically tied to his opposition to the Soviet regime. He shared his understanding of the operation of totalitarian system in the USSR in many of his writings. In his prison memoir, *And the Wind Returns*, he describes the Soviet system of power as follows:

> Its main difference from democratic power is that it does not derive from public opinion. In such a state an individual cannot have any rights; any bit of an intrinsic individual right takes away from the totality of state power. Everyone in such a system has to know from childhood that under no circumstances can an individual influence the authorities. Any decision is initiated from the top. The authorities are unshakable, infallible and inexorable and everyone in the world just has to adapt. One can ask for mercy with humility but cannot demand what's rightful. It does not need citizens concerned with legality; it needs slaves. (Bukovsky 2007: 203)

Bukovsky shares this understanding of how the system crushed individual rights and did not recognize the inherent value of individual lives and thoughts with all the writers discussed in this book so far. Concern about the individual value and self-expression suppressed under communism is a central preoccupation and a source of unhappiness for Miłosz, Markov and Zinoviev.

While at heart ideologically driven, Bukovsky's view of the Soviet man also relied on his personal experiences that undoubtedly biased his general conclusions. In his life of a non-conformist and in the process of his defiant struggle against the system, he often encountered the human element of the system that was responsible for the system's maintenance: the KGB officers, the Soviet judges, the prison guards, the doctors, nurses and lower medical staff in the psychiatric words. Describing the 1972 trial, where Bukovsky was charged with anti-Soviet slander for the materials about Soviet psychiatry he was able to publicize in the West, he writes about the Soviet judges and their role in the system (similar to Hanna Arendt's observations about the banality of evil in her *Eichmann in Jerusalem* (1963):

They wanted to stay clean and did not want to hear about the abuse, murders and dirt [in the psychiatric hospitals]. What relation does it have to them personally? They do not kill themselves, do not strangle people in 'ukrutkas,' do not break spines, and do not trample and kick with their boots. They only move papers, put their signatures and stamp documents. What comes out of it is of no concern to them. They live in comfort and sleep well at night (314). [. . .] That's how they work: some torture trying to get confessions and others are trying to moralize, ask callous questions. (315)

Similar to Zinoviev, Bukovsky believed that most of the Soviet society was integrated into this system of violence and shared sincere feelings of belonging to the great Soviet state. He viewed the pattern of systemic adaptation as a form of false consciousness.

Everyone, from the Politburo members, academicians and writers to workers and kolkhozniki, find their excuse. Most often people are sincere. Rarely does anyone realize that this is just an excuse. Very few can honestly accept that they are just driven by the fear of repressions. Only once had someone told me that the communist system suits him: it allows him to earn money through publishing all kind of demagoguery trash in the newspapers.[8]

There were only a few groups that fell out of the system. Among these, according to Bukovsky, are the genuine Orthodox sect that branched out from the Orthodox Church and is mostly in prisons. And then, there are homeless, who are also not part of the system.

The rest, whether they want it or not, are building communism. The state does not care which theories they are using to justify their participation, what they think and feel. As long as they do not resist, protest and publicly oppose, they suit the Soviet state. No love is needed. Everything is simple and cynical: do you want a new apartment? Present at a meeting.

Do you want a salary raise of 20-30 rubles, and get a promotion? Become a party member. Are you afraid of losing material benefits and get into trouble? Vote, work and keep silent. Everyone is doing that. No one wants to spit against the wind. This is the real foundation of the state that continues to exterminate people in prison, install fear, enslave other people and threaten the world.[9]

In short, Bukovsky's vision of *Homo Sovieticus* in many ways matched that of Alexander Zinoviev. Very much prompted by their own characters, commitments and challenges of living in a Soviet society and interacting with the system they despised, they have transferred their hatred of the system on the human element (i.e. Soviet people) that they viewed to be the product of adaptation to that system. Of course, they were part and parcel of the Soviet people as well.

Homo Sovieticus as a dissent

All non-conformist intellectuals from different parts of the Soviet bloc, and different national and family backgrounds shared something important in common. They were all children or, in some ways, even prisoners, of their historical epoch of the Cold War. Cold War politics shaped not only *their* views, perceptions and expectations, but also the reception and interpretation of their creative works, especially in the West. All dissident writers discussed above became widely viewed as anti-communist thinkers who contributed to the exposure of totalitarianism and to the important discussions about the impact of the communist system on society and individuals. They were idolized in the West and their fame is very much a reflection of the politics of the era. Just as Miłosz was unhappy about what he was praised for by one of his reviewers, the rest of them could also rightfully complain about the one-sided assessment of their views and the labels attached to them among the broader educated public.

The reality of their lives and the content of their views were more complex and nuanced than were commonly recognized. All four of them faced the necessity of negotiating the double disappointment in their lives: the first one was reflected in the tragedy of their forced decisions to escape their countries following the early career success each one of them experienced. The second disappointment was in and with the West. Their early ideals about the West – the ideals of living in a free and democratic society comprising autonomous individuals – gave way to a painful realization that the West has many of the social and political ills that they rejected in their own countries.

Alexander Zinoviev was perhaps the most expressive of these disappointments when he noted: 'It is truly amazing but every Soviet scoundrel has a negative double in the West' (55). Vladimir Bukovsky, labelled by some observers an 'eternal dissident', also maintained his critical stance in the West. The European Union specifically drew his intense reprehension:

In 2010, as a senior fellow at the Cato Institute, he wrote:

This pattern of dictatorship, oppression, and lack of freedom of speech is rising not only in third world countries, but also in Europe and the United States. Europe faces the emerging monster of the European Union, which looks suspiciously like the Soviet Union in many respects – though admittedly only a pale copy.

Even Georgy Markov and Czeslaw Miłosz, though not such contrarians by character as Zinoviev and Bukovsky, were unhappy with and critical of the capitalist consumerism and individual alienation that they faced in the West. They criticized the communist regimes for not delivering on the promises made by the Party; but also conveyed an appreciation for the fundamental ideas of social justice and common human fate revealing the extent to which the values of socialism made them who they were. They revealed a deep longing for a more spiritual and socially fulfilling lives that they lacked in the West.

Nonetheless, political émigrés with anti-communist views could not escape but play a political role during the Cold War. The views about life under communism provided by the more neutral observers visiting the Soviet Union lacked the sharp criticism associated with the work of the dissidents from the Eastern side of the Iron Curtain.

The more detached approach to Soviet society by those who were not engaged in the domestic struggle with the system produced more sanguine observations about *Homo Sovieticus*. The last part of this chapter will focus on the German political scientist and journalist, Klaus Mehnert, who also wrote a book about *Soviet man*, trying to figure out whether the Bolsheviks delivered on their goal of creating a New Soviet Man.

'The people of the Soviet Union remain, but Stalins come and go . . .'

Born to a Russian-German family in Moscow in 1906, Klaus Mehnert used the term 'Soviet man' (*Der Sowjetmensch*) in his book with the same title published in 1958. The book was translated into English in 1961 with the title *The Anatomy of the Soviet Man*. Based on his personal meetings and conversations with Soviet citizens (especially fruitful ones that occurred on trains and planes), but also relying on literary works, journalist and theatre productions, Mehnert tried to convey the realities of the Soviet everyday life in the 1950s. Mehnert was not pursuing any theoretical ambitions. Fully fluent in Russian given his childhood, he had a personal connection to Russian society and a desire to understand whether the Bolsheviks, who promised to develop a New Soviet Man, were successful in their efforts to change human nature and raise a selfless individual. His book was among the first ones in the West that provided the picture of the Soviet Union during late Stalinism.

One of the contributions of Mehnert's book was to discuss the gap between the Soviet ideological declarations and the real life of ordinary citizens. Contrary to ideological principles propagated by the government, he argued, both at the elite and mass level, Soviet people had 'bourgeois' leanings and were interested in promoting their own economic well-being and consumption as opposed to advancing the societal goals. The difference with the Western public was that the Soviets had to do it within the framework of the Communist regime, seen as unavoidable and permanent.

Unlike other writings on the Soviet society that were published after Mehnert's book, *Der Sowjetmensch* was not dominated by the totalitarian framework used by many critical observers during the Cold War. Mehnert did mention the totalitarian state but he separated the people from the regime and focused mostly on the society:

> The people of the Soviet Union remain, but the Stalins come and go. And not only the Stalins. (Preface to 1962 translated edition)

Departing from the totalitarian approach, which held that Soviet people were largely atomized because of Stalinist traumas, Mehnert depicted Soviet society and Soviet life as 'uncommonly varied' (p. 57), depending on the different context and environment different individuals and groups experienced it. For the Soviet privileged class, the upper stratum that included enterprise managers and Party officials – life resembled, at least in its appearances, Western life with private offices, secretaries and salaries that were much higher than those of the lower stratum. The workers and peasants, a social group much less accessible to the foreigners, were less understood. Mehnert described this group as having a split personality: 'flattered by the official myth that they are the sector on which the growth of the state is based (. . .) [and] dissatisfied with their standards of living' (68).

At the societal level, Mehnert saw the increasing demands for material well-being and a common desire 'to rise socially and amass power and fortune' (194) – features that made the Soviet society very close to those he knew in the West. He commented on 'the Soviet people's respect for learning' (310) and their 'desire to understand the world' with illustrations of crowded bookshops. Mehnert also dedicated pages of his book to discussing the problems of alcoholism, extreme caution on political issues especially among the upper strata in the society, group conformity and readiness to submit to authority (p. 427).

Mehnert's comprehensive sociological depiction of Soviet society was balanced and neutral in its intent. His possession of cultural and linguistic resources was unmatched and extremely helpful, no doubt. It is of course important to remember that these were observations of a person who was raised as a child in pre-Soviet Russia and the nostalgic longing for his childhood years in Russia might have provided a sentimental background for many of his human encounters in Soviet Russia. After all, Mehnert did not live in the Soviet Union. He spent some limited time travelling, observing and reporting from the Soviet Union; but he experienced the country from his privileged position of a foreigner. The special treatment reserved for foreigners he described in detail in his book. Nonetheless, given the diversity and breadth of his encounters and experiences across the Soviet Union's vast territory and diverse social groups, it is hard to imagine that a childhood nostalgia provided a constant factor for his assessments. His personal background might have provided a general desire to understand the Soviet society from the inside and with a sympathetic eye, but his professional instincts of a political scientist and a journalist have undoubtedly guided his conclusions as well.

Observing such striking differences in views of *Homo Sovieticus* of critical insiders forced to emigrate and the more neutral outsiders who wanted to understand the social changes in the USSR highlights the role of politics in the circulation of dominant ideas of the times. Political struggles and victories are crucial for how we perceive and interpret facts. History is always written retrospectively. As the Soviet Union stepped on the path of reforms, the anti-communist position that prevailed in the West (along with its views of *Homo Sovieticus*) was adopted by the reform-minded intellectuals and policymakers in the late Soviet Union.

CHAPTER 4
HOMO SOVIETICUS AS A PERESTROIKA CHILD

The ideas associated with dissent in the 1960s–1970s came to rule the day in the late 1980s, when perestroika and glasnost opened the floodgates of change. Inside the USSR, the term *Homo Sovieticus* obtained academic credentials and more robust analytical and methodological underpinnings. Yuri Levada, a Soviet and Russian sociologist whose name was memorialized through the founding of the Levada Center, developed a systematic methodology and an empirical grounding for a new conceptual category they labelled an 'ordinary Soviet person'. Levada Center is today one of the last independent pollsters in Russia that not only proudly carries Levada's name but also continues his scholarly legacy under the increasing pressure from the government.

Yuri Levada was from the cohort of Soviet sociologists born around the late 1920s. This group includes such intellectual heavyweights as Vladimir Yadov, Boris Grushin, Igor Kon, Gennady Ossipov and Tatiana Zaslavskaya. These scholars in effect founded Soviet sociology – a discipline that had to navigate between the strict principles of historical materialism imposed as the ideological and epistemological basis of the Soviet regime and the pragmatic necessity of dealing with the entrenched social problems in the country. They received massive public acclaim in the 1990s and 2000s but their professional careers in the Soviet period were at times much rockier than the fame they enjoyed later.

Soviet sociology

Soviet sociologists did not have it easy. Sociology was declared 'a bourgeois science' and purged entirely during the Stalin era, replaced instead by the historical materialist philosophy and scientific communism. Until the last years of the Soviet Union the country's universities did not have sociology departments. Most of the intellectual stars in Soviet sociology were, according to Vladimir Yadov, himself a star of Soviet sociology, 'self-made sociologists' (Firsov 2012).

The discipline experienced a revival during the late 1950s and 1960s. The official recognition of sociology as a discipline occurred in 1958, when the Soviet authorities were pressured to set up the Soviet Sociological Association (SSA) to enable Soviet attendance at international conferences. Participation in such international symposia was considered to be a matter of prestige as well as ideological necessity: the conferences were the spaces in which the Soviet scientists could oppose, expose and denounce capitalist theories, while defending the socialist project. Developing a scientific basis for demonstrating the advantages of socialism was the primary objective of creating the SSA (Bikbov and Gavrilenko 2003: 55). These developments also meant that the Soviet establishment had to enable at least a selected group of scholars to follow the developments in Western social sciences and read Western sociologists.

Nonetheless, Soviet sociology remained a highly protected field of knowledge and was quite unique in terms of its place in the ideological machine that propped up the Soviet system. A central legitimating myth of Soviet society posited that it developed according to objective historical laws and particularly evolved according to a scientifically devised plan (Sokolov 2017). Marxist-Leninist ideology predicted specific social processes such as a gradual elimination of the social and cultural gap between the intelligentsia and the working class; and assumed political processes such as the Soviet peoples' support for the Party. In light of these expectations, any accurate information about the real state of social development in the Soviet Union had implications for the legitimacy of the regime as a whole (Sokolov 2017: 192). The authorities had to be ideologically and politically creative to deal with unfulfilled predictions. The state's control over the information helped. As a common way of dealing with these issues, the government simply suppressed real facts about Soviet society. Most statistical and demographic information was classified and any information that could be used to discredit the system was carefully guarded.[1]

In the 1960s and 1970s, the Soviet state charged sociologists with developing a rationalized and scientific vision of the Soviet social development. Post-war developments in Western empirical sociology opened greater spaces for discussions about rationalization, social engineering and social planning. The Soviet state already planned all economic activities in the country through Gosplan. Now social scientists could advocate for the scientifically driven social development and for including social development parameters into the big Plan (Sokolov 2017: 196). 'Scientific organization of labor' and 'social planning' became the catchwords driving all-Union campaigns during the 1970s (Sokolov 2017: 195).

Soviet sociologists had to adhere to the Marxist-Leninist paradigm and assume its correctness. This ideological restriction meant that they faced severe constraints in their capacity to undertake empirical research. The Soviet Union did not have any research centres that were allowed to do nation-wide surveys. All sociological studies were restricted to small spaces such as a specific enterprise, a small town or a village, so that the empirical results not corroborating the grand theory could be presented as an aberration or a special case that did not discredit the Soviet system at large. Large-scale comprehensive studies were considered too dangerous from the ideological perspective.

The sociological studies therefore all carried an applied character. Scholars were expected to focus on concrete problems of Soviet society and devise solutions. The problems of social nature in the socialist system were a plenty including such issues as work discipline and low productivity. The solutions focused on the optimization of the management of scientific and technological progress (*nauchno-tekhnicheskii progress*) and regulation of workers' collectives (Bikbov and Gavrilenko 2003: 55). These concrete social problems were articulated by the administrators in the context of specific organizations. This applied and administrative character of Soviet sociology meant that the whole discipline followed the imperative of improving management and regulation of socialist production processes.

Yuri Levada as a Soviet scholar

Yuri Levada was one of the young scholars who did get access to Western theories. Born in Belarus in 1930, Levada joined the Soviet sociological establishment after graduating from the philosophy department of the Moscow State University in 1952 and defending his candidacy of science dissertation in 1955. He initially conducted some sociological studies in China but the worsening Sino-Soviet relations made this work more complicated. During the 1960s Levada explored the sociology of religion and gave lectures on sociology at the Department of Journalism of the Moscow State University. In the mid-1960s Levada joined a group of scholars at the Philosophy Institute of the Academy of Science that later, in 1968, founded the Institute for Applied Sociological Studies (IKSI). This was the first scholarly group in the Soviet Union that worked on developing an autonomous sociological analysis in a relatively independent fashion.

IKSI was a short-lived product of the Thaw era. Levada himself noted that the Soviet regime was somewhat 'undecided' about its continued survival during the early Brezhnev period (Levada 2006: 116). This brief opening ended after the 1968 Prague Spring and the subsequent clampdown in Czechoslovakia. Soon after IKSI's founding the Soviet authorities went after liberal niches in Soviet academia. Levada's sociology lectures that were published in 1969 were used as a pretext for an intellectual purge at IKSI. Levada was accused of political and ideological mistakes, pressured to admit to his mistakes and given a 'reprimand' (*vygovor*) – one of the disciplining measures used by the CPSU. He lost his position at Moscow State University but was able to keep his job at the Institute until 1972, when a change in its leadership pressured him to leave. This purge at IKSI became the sign of things to come in other places. Similar politically driven campaigns later took place at research centres in Tartu, Leningrad and Novosibirsk (Sokolov 2017: 197).

Levada's professional life in the 1970s – up until the changes brought by Gorbachev's reforms in the 1980s – was a great illustration of the anthropologist Alexei Yurchak's analysis in *Everything Was Forever Until It Was No More* (2013). Going against the mainstream analysis of the Brezhnev era that focused on the oppressive state and resisting (or pliant) society, Yurchak highlighted the role of unofficial and largely autonomous spaces allowed by the late Soviet state. In them Soviet citizens could develop ideas and practices that did not fit the rigid and hollow ideological shell of Marxism-Leninism. He termed this phenomenon 'de-territorialized milieu' or living 'vnye' (outside the system). The official 'shell' constituted by formal institutional routines, slogans, practices and rhetoric was recognized by the majority as an unescapable formality and part of life, but it was often not relevant for individual cultural and professional aspirations and interests. These interests were pursued outside this official realm. In the 1970s these autonomous spaces were referred to as 'the second science' and 'the second art' (Levada 2006: 117). Small communities of artists and scientists gathered in different flats, kitchens and basements constituting a dynamic underground life that was for the most part tolerated by the regime. The vibrancy of such 'kitchen' life, the values, authenticity and communality present in such informal spaces in the late Soviet Union is a subject of many memoirs today. That parallel intellectual and cultural life was most intense in the capital and other big cities of the Soviet Union.

After being squeezed out from the Institute of Philosophy Levada found an academic position at the Central Economic Mathematical Institute of the Russian Academy of Science (CEMI) and focused on the sociology of economic development. The real and exciting scholarly life however took place outside CEMI. Levada was in the centre of the group organizing regular, informal academic seminars *dlya svoikh* (for those who are 'in'), which at times expanded to an audience of 200–300 and at other times remained as a small informal circle (Levada 2006: 117). This was the place where the more independent-thinking Soviet scholars who wanted to work outside the rigid boundaries of Marxist orthodoxy could discuss new ideas and trends in sociology, psychology, semiotics and cultural studies.

They were not engaged with Western scholars but did read Western literature. Later, in an interview, Levada mentioned discussing works by Max Weber, Talcott Parsons and Emile Durkheim, Claude Levi-Strauss and George Murdoch. He also noted the importance of works by such Russian scholars as Vyacheslav Ivanov, Vladimir Toporov and Aleksandr Pyatigorsky – all associated with Yuri Lotman's Tartu-Moscow school of semiotics, itself one of the islands of intellectual freedom that emerged at the time of political 'thaw' in the Soviet Union.[2] These Soviet scholars who participated in these seminars in Levada's admission, played a big role in creating individuals who could think independently and creatively (Levada 2006: 118).

With the exception of the Tartu-Moscow school, these seminars did not produce new theories and new scholarly traditions. Instead, they played a role of inspirational venues for those intellectuals who really valued scholarly exploration but were surrounded by the stifling atmosphere of a heavily censored and bureaucratized Soviet sciences. Such unofficial intellectual circles also sprang up in St Petersburg and Novosibirsk and involved other disciplines.

Perestroika and the need for new sociology

Mikhail Sokolov, a sociologist at the European University in St. Petersburg, has noted how many of Soviet sociology's heavyweights experienced delayed recognition. Their Soviet intellectual legacies went into oblivion, while their work in the last years of the Soviet Union and in the 1990s received the greatest number of citations and gained them public fame approximating a cult of personality (2017). As with many of these intellectuals born around 1927–30, Yuri Levada's sociological star has also risen during the perestroika and in the 1990s. How did that happen?

Sokolov suggested that this delayed recognition was linked to the specific conditions of 'intentional secrecy' imposed by the Soviet system. Soviet scholars had to negotiate and devise ways of pursuing important research in the conditions when such research was dangerous because of its implications for the system. 'The reason why they were so repressed', Sokolov argues, 'was precisely because what they said was considered so important' (Sokolov 2017: 204).[3]

Perestroika and the reforms of the Soviet system that were initiated by Mikhail Gorbachev became a great opening for a more autonomous sociological research. Gorbachev highlighted the need to activate the role of the masses in the sociopolitical processes in the country. Engaging the public in government processes was seen as a crucial component for the system's successful renewal. In these new conditions the study of public opinion at the Union level became an essential part of the project of creating the feedback mechanisms necessary to renew the system.

The 1987 establishment of the All-Union Center for the Study of Public Opinion (VTsIOM) was one of the institutional responses to that need. VTsIOM was established under the Soviet Trade Union (VTsSPS) patronage. A well-known sociologist from Novosibirsk, Tatiana Zaslavskaya, was invited to head the organization that became the leading Soviet and then Russian center for the study of public opinion. The analysis based on VTsIOM surveys was published in the journal *Public Opinion Monitoring* (*Monitoring obshchestvennogo mnenia*) that was founded in 1992. Zaslavskaia invited Yuri Levada and his group to join the organization. In 1988 Levada became the head of VTsIOM's theoretical research department. It is at this historical moment of the last years of the Soviet Union that Levada finally obtained the resources necessary for realizing his long-held aspirations for the empirically driven sociological study of Soviet society. Without delay, his group developed a grand proposal to study 'an ordinary Soviet man', a project that went into the field in 1989.

Yuri Levada as 'Professor Preobrazhensky'

Russian literature has a well-known character, Professor Preobrazhensky, a surgeon from Mikhail Bulgakov's *Heart of a Dog* (*Sobach'e serdtse*, 1924), who transplanted an element of a human brain and human testicles into a stray dog, causing a gradual transformation of the dog into a primitive human being. Through the character of Professor Preobrazhensky Bulgakov criticized human arrogance of interfering with nature and trying to transform it through experimentation and human action. The ideas of 'human enhancement' through genetic selection were popular in the United States and in Europe in the early twentieth century. Known as the eugenics movement, they reached the Soviet Union as well, where they merged with the Bolshevik project of creating a New Man.

The character of Professor Preobrazhensky – who became an icon in Soviet popular culture – received heightened media attention in Russia few years back. A public opinion poll conducted by VTsIOM in 2019 revealed a growing appreciation for this character reflected in responses to the question: which of the following movie characters do you associate with an ideal political leader? Preobrazhensky was the second most popular selection after Stirlitz, a Soviet spy from the popular Soviet television series, *Seventeen Moments of Spring* (1973). While Stirlitz was the most popular character nation-wide, Professor Preobrazhensky was the top selection for the residents of Moscow and St. Petersburg. The image of a successful intellectual who is dedicated to his profession, unhappy with the surrounding system, but not ready to act against it resonated in Russia's two biggest cities (Tyazhlov and Galanina 2019). Professor Preobrazhensky was an anti-Bolshevik who did not care to hide his views; yet he was also untouchable because high-ranking officials relied on his professional help.

There are some interesting parallels between Yuri Levada and Professor Preobrazhensky, even if their scientific affiliations were different. Both wanted to understand human beings. Both seemed somewhat sceptical of people surrounding them and looked at a human being as a product of outside forces. Both shared a faith in social engineering. The only difference was that Professor Preobrazhensky was involved in that engineering himself, experimenting with human and animal biology. Yuri Levada, on the other hand, was concerned particularly with how the totalitarian system changed human nature, creating a new species, *Homo Sovieticus*. Preobrazhensky (or, rather, Bulgakov) was looking at Soviet society at its early formation stages. Levada examined the Soviet person as an output of the system as well as the element contributing to its sustainability.

In a public lecture from 2004, Levada noted that he was driven by the problem of an individual or person (*problema cheloveka*) in the preceding fifteen years of his life and his work. Well positioned to study the late Soviet man with the newly available resources, Levada and his close associates including Lev Gudkov, Boris Dubin and Alexei Levinson, developed in 1989 a massive research project 'Soviet person'. They planned it to develop a portrait of the Soviet person at the moment of the decomposition of the Soviet political system. The 'Soviet man' project is undoubtedly Levada's magnum opus. He was the undisputable intellectual leader providing its main vision and organizing the collective work.

This massive research project involved nation-wide public opinion surveys conducted in 1989–90 – the years preceding the fall of the Soviet Union. One of the practical aims of this project was to investigate whether the Soviet people were ready for the democratic reforms that were initiated by Gorbachev. The findings were critical and reflected Levada's own political convictions and potential insecurities about the pace and prospects of democratization in the country.

The anatomy of the Soviet man: What did Levada discover?

The survey questionnaires included about a hundred questions about individual attitudes towards family, work, religion, tradition, violence and love as well as political attitudes and predispositions. The survey covered a representative sample of 2,700 respondents in various parts of the country. The first results of this project were published in a 1993 collective monograph, *A Soviet Ordinary Person* (*Sovetskii Prostoi Chelovek*).

The resulting portrait of the Soviet man based on these surveys was not attractive. The conceptualized *Soviet personality* was found to comprise four core features: (1) forced self-isolation/exceptionalism, (2) state paternalism, (3) egalitarian hierarchism and (4) imperial syndrome. Revealing both their Soviet training and the turbulent times when this project was implemented, Levada's team involved a dialectical approach to create their four categories.[4] Each of the characteristics they highlighted in the Soviet personality had its co-existing opposite. They were *antinomies* – contradictory principles both valid simultaneously. The two parts of the antinomy were not necessarily equal: one element was more dominant and visible, while the opposite feature was more latent. Levada's framework asserted that the more visible element dominated during the periods of stability of the system. The latent elements surfaced when the system weakened, turning into a strong destabilizing force and revealing the purported role of Soviet personality in system maintenance (p. 24).

These antinomies were seen as important because, as Levada later shared, they viewed the Soviet man as a dying species that was in the process of decomposition. The Soviet system was unfolding. Although scholars did not quite predict that the Soviet state would collapse, they did see its fragility and realized that Gorbachev's reforms were undermining its core pillars. Therefore, they tried to account for both the ongoing political and social changes unleashed by perestroika and glasnost and the widely perceived stability of the system. The Soviet-style training in dialectics (something we could already see in dissident writings, especially that of Zinoviev), once again proved its usefulness in this project. Let us now go over each of the traits of the Soviet man that were deemed important by the Levada team.

The first antinomy – forced self-isolation – referred to Soviet man's sense of exceptionalism associated with the state propaganda of Soviet exceptionalism and superiority. A Soviet person believed himself to be a special person – a human container and a micro-reflection of the exceptionalism of the Soviet state. A Soviet person was a carrier of special, Soviet values. Soviet scientific, cultural and social institutions formed as an alternative to bourgeois institutions, Soviet literature, art and education – all worked to inculcate Soviet citizens with a particular system of ethical and aesthetical standards and categories that were presumed to be superior to those elsewhere and worthy of a wider transmission.

The contradicting element in this antinomy, according to Levada's team, was that the sense of Soviet exceptionalism could have positive or negative valence depending on the context. The special Soviet way – whether in the form of various institutions such as education and science or government policies such as the 'world piece agenda' (*mir vo vsem mire*) central to the rhetoric of the late Soviet state – was normally seen as superior to others. At times, though, the perceptions of the special character of Soviet institutions and practices turned upside down, painting everything Soviet in a negative light and presenting Soviet things as inferior relative to the rest of the world. Levada saw these self-denigrating tendencies expressed through the widely circulating term 'sovok' as part of the Soviet exceptionalism syndrome (even if expressed in such an inverted format).

Levada's sociologists recognized that the Soviet government could not counter a growing public realization in the late Soviet period that Western countries have long superseded the Soviet Union in terms of development. The late Soviet admiration for Western clothing and especially jeans – a favourite article for speculators (*fartsovshchiki*), the widespread appeal of Western music, cinema and many consumer items (even those exported from Romania, East Germany and Bulgaria) – all reflected the attractiveness of non-Soviet goods and reminded of the inferiority of the consumer items produced in the planned Soviet economy. After all, some favourite Soviet items such as Soviet 'Lada' (or *zhiguli*) or even the sorely missed Soviet ice cream (*plombir*) – were all created at first as replicas of their Western counterparts (the Italian Fiat in the case of Lada and the American ice cream that was selected by the Soviet leader Anastas Mikoyan during his trip to the United States in 1936 along with the technology for producing it).[5] By the 1970 and 1980s these products were perceived to be authentically Soviet. The aspirations of many Soviet citizens were still directed Westward as people invested their energy to getting luxury products such as furniture produced in Romania, boots produced in Yugoslavia and perfume produced in Bulgaria or Latvia.

In the field of ideas, also, the Soviet intelligentsia increasingly turned from 'a regime supporter into a carrier of the Western patterns'. Vasily Aksenov, a Soviet writer, admitted later: 'The picture of America that our generation pieced together in its imagination was impossibly idealized and distorted' (Aksenov 1987: 19). Yuri

Levada's own career trajectory and professional objectives were a good illustration of these trends. This very project on ordinary Soviet man was driven by two analytical frames that were developed by Western scholars. The big difference between Levada and other members of the Soviet intelligentsia was that Levada tried to popularize his Western ideas during the 1960s through his lectures (and was professionally punished for his attempt), while the majority of his peers waited until perestroika and glasnost to go public with them.

The second antinomy, state paternalism, highlighted the overpowering role of the Soviet party-state in the lives of the ordinary people. According to Levada, the Soviet socialist state was totalitarian in its very conception in that it did not leave any autonomous space for the individual (p. 16). Historians and political scientists often argue that the development of strong states is a response to the challenges of modernization and a catch-up development.[6] The Soviet state also undertook a rapid industrialization and modernization of the Soviet economy and society. But Levada noted that the Soviet state was not there for modernization purposes only. He highlighted the 'guardianship' and 'control' functions of the Soviet state and its constant 'paternalist care' for the citizens. The Soviet-style paternalism looked very much as a 'motherly' care though because the fatherly role was left for the national leader (Levada 1993: 16).

Sociological surveys conducted in 1990 revealed that many Soviet citizens expected that the state leaders and even managers of state enterprises show 'care for their people' (*zabota o narode*). The Soviet party-state was the foremost source of such care for the ordinary citizens. It provided social guarantees and constructed 'a cradle-to-grave' welfare system that endowed the citizens with various entitlements including free education, healthcare and universal employment. These entitlements were available to all who did not challenge the political rules and the power of the party. Anyone who did not recognize the superiority of such system was presumed to be 'mentally confused' and in need of mental treatment.

In return, the Soviet people were asked for gratitude along with dedication and work in promoting the lofty goals of the party-state.

This exchange was at the core of the 'moral economy' of the Soviet Union in which the state was presumed 'to dispense necessary goods and services and the tremendously beholden citizens were obligated to provide their labor in return'.[7] Alas, the expected dedication was not there. As the late Soviet saying asserted, 'they pretend to pay us and we pretend to work'. The time of heroic work effort in pursuit of communist future was long over in the last decades of Soviet existence. Nonetheless, the dispositions with regard to what the state owed the Soviet citizens were deeply engrained. Even when the ideological influence of the Soviet state progressively diminished in the late Soviet period, the majority of Soviet citizens (around 60% according to surveys) thought that people could not live without the constant care and guardianship of the state.

The public opinion surveys conducted by the Levada team revealed a growing popular discontent with the amount and quality of care they received. The Soviet system was quickly losing its grounding during 1989–90 as the political and economic reforms pursued by Gorbachev unleashed the political forces that brought the system to its implosion. After the Soviet collapse, the new Russian state was also in the midst of liberal reforms that resulted in the state retreating from many of its earlier obligations. The surveys conducted in 1992 revealed that some 36 per cent of respondents were unsatisfied and thought that the 'care about people' was insufficient and that the state was failing in its functions, creating social insecurity. The Levada team noted that these dispositions highlighted the pervasiveness of paternalist attitudes instilled in the Soviet period.

The third antinomy Yuri Levada thought important to *Homo Sovieticus* was 'hierarchical egalitarianism', as he labelled it. It brought attention to the simultaneity of Soviet citizens' acceptance of egalitarian ideals that rejected inequalities along with the acceptance of selected hierarchies (and inequalities) derived from the paternalist state organization. While postulating the equality of all Soviet people, the Soviet system extended privileges to those who occupied important state positions. These processes produced an unequal, socially stratified society with the privileged *nomenklatura* system comprising important state and party positions.

Michael Voslensky, a Soviet historian who defected to the West, referred to nomenklatura as the new Soviet ruling class (1984). The privileges shared by nomenklatura involved access to special healthcare centres as well as access to goods that were not accessible to ordinary citizens through special stores and service centres. These privileges turned into a significant source of popular resentment during the perestroika and a subject of populist critique used by politicians for mobilizing popular support. Boris Yeltsin, Russia's first president, rose to power riding on the coat-tails of intense anti-nomenklatura sentiments that engulfed Soviet society in the late 1980s.

Levada's fourth antinomy highlighted the co-existence of rising nationalist sentiments in the Soviet Union with the internationalist principles that were at the foundation of the Soviet State and were central to the Soviet ideology. Levada referred to this feature as an imperial character of *Homo Sovieticus* (also using the term 'imperial syndrome') and viewed it as a main source of tension that brought about the Soviet collapse (Levada 1993: 22). *Homo Sovieticus* is 'genetically frustrated because he faces an impossible task of choosing between his ethnic and supra-national belonging' (Levada 1993).

The rising social tensions in the late Soviet Union were reflected in the growing nationalist tensions that, in the end, produced an ethnic explosion in the late 1980s. The long-promoted internationalist orientations clashed in the late Soviet period with the consolidating national identities producing a growing demand for a greater autonomy from Moscow on the part of national peripheries. The myth about the brotherly unity of the Soviet people was exposed to be a lie. The opinion polls conducted in the context of the project on Soviet personality showed that only 25 per cent of the Soviet people were proud to be Soviet citizens.

In Levada's thinking these four central features of the Soviet man were typical and dominant, even if not universally applicable to every Soviet citizen. Levada sociologists believed that in its classical format these features were produced and expressed most fully at the height of Stalinism during the 1930s–1940s. By 1989–91, when the surveys were conducted, these features were presumably in the process of degradation.

Besides these four core personality features, Levada discussed the soviet person's simplicity (*prostota*). While I translated the word 'prostoi' used in the title of Levada's research project as 'ordinary', to highlight its reference to commonality, ordinariness and the non-elite nature of the category of people these sociologists tried to describe, 'prostoi' could also be translated as simple. Levada team meant many things by 'prostoi': a Soviet person was a person of the masses (one of many) and faced a strong pressure to conform; a Soviet person was opposed to elitism and any exceptional success or achievement; a Soviet person was ascetic and oriented towards survival (but not any luxury); a Soviet person was simple and transparent (i.e. easy to understand, uncomplicated) (Levada 1993: 24–6).

These opinion polls also highlighted the atomization of the Soviet society, allowing the Levada team to rebuff the common beliefs about Soviet collectivism. They wrote:

> We just did not discover this feature [collectivism]. No social-psychological communities associated with a profession, hobbies or interests stood between the totalitarian state and a lonely individual. The party-state machinery of power was the practical carrier of the collective 'we.'

These observations resonated with Hannah Arendt's analysis of atomized, isolated individuals who Arendt viewed as the social basis of totalitarianism.[8]

So there you have it: the first-ever systematically conducted sociological study of *Homo Sovieticus* concluded that he was a product of the paradoxes the Soviet experience fostered. The conditions of individual survival in the context of the totalitarian state, according to Levada, demanded and depended on a sort of a 'pact with the devil' and the emergent 'games' between the Soviet citizens and the system of power in which each side played a specific role. These expectations and adaptations reflected and produced the system of double-standards and hypocrisy that Levada compared to Orwellian doublethinking. Just like the anti-communist dissidents, Levada's team deemed these trends to be destructive of the ethical foundations of human personality (Levada 1993: 32). It is this moral judgement that, arguably, hid the political stance of the writers and scholars who arrived at it represented the harshest accusation against the ordinary Soviet man.

Levada's analytical tools

The head of the theoretical department at VTsIOM, Yuri Levada was the analytical mastermind of the Soviet man project. More than a decade after Levada's departure (he died of a heart attack in 2006), his colleagues at the Levada Center still work within the analytical frame he developed. Its continuing relevance – it is by far the most-respected opinion poll center in Russia today[9] – makes it that much more urgent to deconstruct and explore the foundations, sources and origins of Levada's analytical toolbox. As in the case with the dissidents discussed in the first chapter, Levada's ideas were the product of his time and his individual intellectual strivings that went well beyond the official boundaries of the Soviet-style social sciences.

The main theoretical construction of this research project relied on two central analytical paradigms. The first – *structural functionalism* – is an approach developed by Talcott Parsons, an influential American sociologist, whose theories of social action came to dominate sociological analysis in the West around the 1950s. Parsons published his most famous books: *The Structure of Social Action* in 1937 and *The Social System* in 1951. His academic fame started reaching the Soviet Union by the late 1950s although only a few Soviet scholars working in St. Petersburg and Moscow, who had a rare chance of interacting with Western scholars, could really follow the theoretical trends developing in the West. A Harvard Professor, Talcott Parsons visited the USSR in 1964, as part of the American delegation. He shared his impressions from that visit in his 1965 article where he asserted that the academic dialogue between the American and Soviet sociologists is possible, the Soviet adherence to Marxism notwithstanding (Parsons 1965).

Structural functionalism developed a view of society as a *system* that has boundaries delimiting the ins and outs of the system. A system's interdependent parts function together and are usually in equilibrium. A social system relies on certain individual value orientations in order for it to survive and continually reproduce. These systemic needs were defined as functional pre-requisites, with the main ones being adaptation, goal attainment, integration and reproduction (or pattern maintenance). Individuals in this theory are born into the system and are a product of social influences around them (family, school, religion, media). They carry out actions that maintain order and enable systemic reproduction. Value orientations in the system could be of a democratic or a non-democratic type. The American system of democracy was taken as an ideal expression of the values associated with the democratic pole. The German National Socialism and Soviet communism exemplified the opposite pole.

Parson's functionalism came under increasing attack in the West during the 1960s and was ultimately discredited as conservative and equilibrium oriented, with no satisfactory explanation of the sources of social change. It did have a longer staying effect in the Soviet Union, however, and it is intriguing to ponder why that was the case and why its impact on Soviet scholars, who were looking for alternatives to the Marxist orthodoxy, was more fundamental. The reasons are likely more than one.

The Soviet sociologists might have been captivated by the Parsonian thinking on society due to its *systemic* nature. Structural functionalism reiterated certain analytical patterns the Soviet education propagated through Marxism-Leninism. In addition, it was a real alternative to Marxist thinking because it offered an understanding of Soviet stagnation and perceived permanence of the Soviet system. The systemic approach to the analysis of social issues and a penchant for broad, all-encompassing theories could be viewed as a cultural trait of Soviet academia. Soviet scholars were taught to think dialectically in terms of interdependent and opposing parts of the whole system. But if the dialectical approach posited conflict to be the element in the system that generates political and social change, the Parsonian approach removed conflict and change from the analysis, while highlighting the reproduction of the consensus and homeostasis (or equilibrium) of the system. The fundamental vision of society as a system with interdependent parts was shared; only the ultimate focus shifted from explaining change to explaining stability. Therefore, Parson's theory was both *legible* in the analytical coordinates that the Soviet scholars were raised and new, more pertinent, at the same time.

The larger political environment in the Soviet Union and the restricted access to information played their role too. The developments in American sociology in the 1950–1960s were more accessible in the Soviet Union during the Thaw period. The debates that ensued in Western academia later, in the 1960s and 1970s, occurred at a time of a conservative closure in the Soviet Union, when those who sought analytical alternatives to Marxism and revealed their interest in 'bourgeois theories' were pressured and removed from their positions. The new ideas that entered Soviet academia in the 1960s, therefore, could not be integrated in empirical research on Soviet society in constructive ways. Nonetheless, the Parsonian-style systemic thinking had a special pertinence in the late Soviet context characterized by the increasing inertia of the Brezhnev period and the practices of social adaptation to solidified institutional forms and structures. It was rather ironic that these ideas waited for their empirical application and their real impact on Soviet science until Gorbachev's reforms, a time of change and turbulence that brought the system to its end. A theory intended to explain stasis and adaptation could only be used at the moment of cataclysmic changes.

The second analytical pillar of Levada's project relied on another Western theory – *totalitarianism*. Levada's research project on the Soviet man is impossible to understand outside the totalitarian model of the Soviet society that provided scholars with terms, categories and a broader vision that guided their interpretation of empirical findings.

The term 'totalitarianism' was first used to refer to Italian fascism in the 1920 and 1930s (Geyer and Fitzpatrick 2009: 3). As an analytical model grouping together fascism and communism it was developed in its classical version by Hannah Arendt in *The Origins of Totalitarianism* (1951) and Carl Friedrich and Zbigniew Brzezinski in their 1956 book *Totalitarian Dictatorship and Autocracy.* Arendt argued that totalitarian regimes 'operated according to a system of values so radically different from all others that none of our traditional legal, moral, or common sense utilitarian categories could any longer help us come to terms with, or judge, or predict their course of action' (Arendt 1973: 460). A model of totalitarianism developed by Friedrich and Brzezinski highlighted the central institutional features of such regimes. They were to include: (1) a single political party controlling the military and the state, (2) an official ideology and control over mass communications, (3) leadership cult, (4) centralized control over the economy and (5) state terror through secret police.

These conceptualizations of totalitarianism turned into a major interpretive lens that guided much political analysis and policy-making during the Cold War. Political opposition between the United States and the Soviet Union resulted in the politicization of analytical categories as well. The Cold War thereby turned into the opposition between totalitarian regimes and the free world exemplified by liberal democracies.

Already in the 1970s a number of Sovietologists challenged the model of totalitarianism, employing instead a modernization approach to interpret Soviet experience (Geyer and Fitzpatrick 2009). Some political scientists even expected the eventual convergence of Soviet and American political systems (Geyer and Fitzpatrick 2009). Andrei Sakharov, a Soviet nuclear physicist and a human rights activist, developed the idea of convergence between the opposing systems of capitalism and socialism in his 1968 essay 'Thoughts on Peace, Progress and Intellectual Freedom'. The totalitarian approach came under the increasing scrutiny after the end of the Cold War, too, and is considered to be outdated by many social scientists and historians in the West. Yet it is an important analytical foundation of the Soviet man project and therefore deserves our attention here.

The collapse of the Soviet Union and the political transitions of the Soviet satellite-states embracing liberal democracy and capitalism reinforced the model of totalitarianism giving rise to the post-communist euphoria and producing the 'end of history' discourse. Anti-communist frames, concepts and categories came to dominate in the late Soviet Union as 'the floodgates opened' during perestroika (Geyer and Fitzpatrick 2009). George Orwell's *1984*, for example, was published by *Novyi Mir* in 1989. Of course, selected Soviet intellectuals, including people like Yuri Levada, were exposed to these ideas already in the 1950 and 1960s. In a brief essay commemorating the centenary of Orwell's birth, Levada remembers that Orwell's *1984* distributed in the 1950s in few, self-printed carbon copies were a 'long-awaited ray of light in the darkness of our past'.

Up until the politics of glasnost, totalitarianism was a taboo subject in the Soviet Union although the concept was known and used in informal communication (Zaslavsky 2002). Its public discussion in the country started in the late 1980s with literary and cinematographic works dedicated to the Stalinist period. Tengiz Abuladze's film *Repentance* (1988) was one of the first cinematographic anti-Stalinist and anti-totalitarian statements in the Soviet Union.

Literary publications in Soviet 'thick journals' that traditionally played a role of the center of cultural and intellectual life in the country were another platform for public debates.

Thick journals flourished during the Thaw, when the literary environment enjoyed considerable autonomy and hundreds of thousands of Soviet citizens of different generations engaged in an 'epic reassessment' of Stalin's legacy following the processes initiated by Nikita Khrushchev (Kozlov 2013: 7). Alexander Solzhenitsyn's *One Day in the Life of Ivan Denisovich* published in 1962, and Ilya Ehrenburg memoir *People, Years, Life* published in the early 1960s became literary watersheds after which many people looked at Soviet history through the prism of the state terror in the 1930s.

The ideas and language elaborated during the Thaw returned to the public realm with the glasnost of the late 1980s. Many anti-Stalinist literary works were published in *Novyi Mir* and *Oktiabr'* in 1987 and 1988 including novels, stories and poems by Anatoly Pristavkin, Daniil Granin, Oleg Dudintsev, Aleksandr Rybakov, Boris Pilniak, Aleksandr Tvardovsky, Nikolai Zabolotsky, Olga Berggolts and many others. Most of them were written decades before and had to wait for this political opening to see the light of the day and reach their audiences.

Boris Pasternak's *Doctor Zhivago*, a Nobel Prize–winning novel, first published in Italy in 1957, was only published in the Soviet Union in 1988. Vasily Grossman's epic *Life and Fate* also was published in

1988 by *Oktiabr'* magazine. Evgenia Ginzburg's *A Journey Into the Whirlwind (Krutoi marshrut)* and Varlam Shalamov's *Kolyma Tales* – both autobiographic testimonies about surviving through the terror and the Stalinist Gulag – were also published around the same time.

Intense public discussions around these publications brought the tragic history of Stalinism into renewed focus. The concept of totalitarianism turned into a media catchword to connote the Stalinist system. It entered the late Soviet political lexicon and was used by Mikhail Gorbachev and then, later, by Boris Yeltsin. While part of the anti-communist lexicon in Russia, the model of totalitarianism did not get any original analytical treatment in Soviet and Russian academia. To the contrary, it seems that much of the pre-existing academic establishment in Russia did not accept its basic model, which postulated a similarity between the Soviet system and that of Nazi Germany (Zaslavsky 2002; Gudkov 2001a).

For Yuri Levada and his team, who welcomed Gorbachev's political reforms and who gained recognition in the late Soviet period, the concept of totalitarianism represented the analytical lens underlying their broader worldview and their attitudes towards the Soviet system. They supported political changes in their country. Their professional work was driven by the new opportunities and reflected their political stance along with the analytical preferences they have developed earlier.

The concept of totalitarianism and the view that the Soviet system was 'on the wrong side of history' combined with Parson's structural functionalism represented the two foundational pillars of Levada's research project on the Soviet man. The totalitarianism pillar was more assumed than discussed in that moment. Ironically, it was the moment when this model was going out of fashion in the West. But in the Soviet Union it represented the *zeitgast* of the historical moment and was taken for granted by politically engaged scholars who viewed themselves to be on the 'right side of history'. Such mixing of the political, the ethical and the analytical created 'a blind spot' that many scholars did not see.

Lev Gudkov, one of Levada's closest associates, attempted to rectify this analytical shortcoming later. In a series of articles published in 2001 he defended the totalitarian model and asserted that the Soviet society came closest to embodying it. He did admit that the origins of the term were associated with the period of the Cold War and the geopolitical and ideological opposition between the Soviet Union and the United States. Nonetheless, Gudkov argued that the model was still relevant in post-Soviet Russia because totalitarianism left important legacies in terms of social relations and organization, identity-building mechanisms and other practices that continued to play an important role in contemporary Russia (2001b).

The Levada Center, continues to view contemporary Russian society through the lens of totalitarianism and Parson's system theory. Yuri Levada's intellectual legacy that builds on Cold-War-era theoretical advancements, which have been superseded in the country of their origin, is rarely questioned. There are scholars who bring attention to these issues. Misha Gabowitsch, a sociologist and historian based at the Einstein Forum in Potsdam (Germany), has long called for a more serious discussion of Levada's intellectual legacy. He complained that the numerous texts commemorating Levada (who died in 2006, at the age of seventy-six) do not pay sufficient attention to Levada's method and theoretical position, instead highlighting his non-conformism, leadership and ethical stance (Gabowitsch 2008: 51). The reasons are understandable. The association of Levada's analytical stance with the 'moral' and 'good' side meant that any substantive, analytical criticism of the theoretical foundation has been hard to come by. Levada's own associates worked to codify Levada's legacy rather than engage with it critically and develop it in new directions. 'It is simpler to mention Levada's great moral authority, as opposed to engage with his theses', Gabowitsch has concluded (Gabowitsch 2008: 55).

Levada's project is very much part of the contemporary media discourse about Russia. Masha Gessen's much acclaimed volume, *The Future Is History* (2017) builds on Levada's *Homo Sovieticus* concept to inquire into Russia's contemporary 'totalitarianism-lite' system erected under Vladimir's Putin's leadership. Gessen's core message is that the entire Russian society is psychologically damaged and unwilling to come to terms with its past. This striking pronouncement labelling an entire society with the use of ideas from the 1950s is lamentable in the least. Journalists are not scientists and are not required to keep up with all the scientific innovation. As I noted in Chapter 1, some ideas are more impressionable and persistent than others in particular circumstances. Nonetheless, the ideas carry costs.

Levada's notion of *Homo Sovieticus* carries a heavy toll. It fits too easily in the currently rising anti-Russian sentiments around the world understandably provoked by Russia's aggression against Ukraine. As Tom Nichols wrote one month before the invasion in *The Atlantic* magazine:

> The Russians, even in Soviet times, were always in the grip of a paradox in which they saw themselves as both a great empire and a nation of dispossessed victims, and Putin is the prime example of Homo Sovieticus, a product of a system whose view of the world constantly wavered between paranoia and messianism.[10]

Such regurgitation of Cold War concepts in the media means the alienation and estrangement of the Russian society. Even more importantly, it represents shifting blame from the Russian elites to the Russian ordinary people. The elite choices of foreign policy orientation in the name of preserving power and access to rents for the selected group of individuals should be viewed as the responsibility of elites. *Homo Sovieticus* as a concept, that returned to the stage after 2014, draws attention in the wrong direction. It is true that the Russian society needs to keep its elites in check. It also needs to rethink the foundations of Russia's collective identity. These processes would require the enhancement of societal agency and efficacy and would, undoubtedly, require more time. And a more mature conversation about societal agency would involve attending to realities on the ground in Russia today, not in its past. This is a reality of abominable inequality and social degradation in Russia's hinterland, of domestic and state violence used as instruments of power, of a personal dictatorship standing for the system of power crushing any opposition and suppressing the public sphere. These realities are more recent in origin than the Cold War and the Soviet history.

CHAPTER 5
HOMO SOVIETICUS AS A POST-SOVIET EMPATHY

The disciplines of sociology and anthropology both belong to the category of human science, also known in the nineteenth century as 'moral sciences'. When the term came into fashion, the so-called moral sciences were juxtaposed to natural sciences due to the recognition of human agency. Humans can act out of free will rather than external stimulus. Humans can reason and be purposeful. These abilities differentiate the social realm from the realm of nature. Although human society remains the central object of exploration in both sociology and anthropology, they differ in how they approach their questions, and how they collect and analyse the data. Sociologists are more problem-oriented. They aspire to parallel the success of natural sciences that have 'conquered' nature; only, in their case, they want to resolve social problems by contributing to the design of social policy interventions. Anthropologists have been more committed to broader humanistic values, aspiring to *understand* the human condition rather than *explain* and *fix*. They have remained more local, benefitting from immersive research strategies and more critical of the deductive approaches to social research associated with testing the fit of pre-designed concepts and frames on the social reality.

Natalia Kozlova was a sociocultural anthropologist who lived in Moscow and dedicated her life to understanding Soviet society and the Soviet people. Her scholarship is less known than that of Yuri Levada but she advanced an alternative approach to studying the Soviet people. Originally trained as a philosopher (the Soviet social science was dominated by scientific communism), she worked from 1972 at the Institute of Philosophy of the Soviet Academy of Science and defended her doctoral degree on everyday life and social change in 1992. Instead of working on pure theory, as philosophers are often thought of, Kozlova ended up spending most of her time in the archives, reading family letters, postcards and diaries written by Soviet people. She used these texts, along with her own experience of living in the Soviet Union, to understand Soviet society and the Soviet person in her everyday life.

Kozlova's intellectual quest trailed that of Yuri Levada, who worked on developing the ideal type of the Soviet person. Contrary to Levada's sociological inquiry that involved Parson's systems theory and totalitarianism, Kozlova relied on a very different analytical foundation combining it with her own 'participatory' knowledge of the people and life in the Soviet period. What for Levada looked like totalitarian inclinations towards 'doublethinking', 'simplicity' and 'adaptability', Kozlova viewed through the lens of French theorist Michel de Certeau's practices and tactics of the everyday life that allow the less powerful members of society to resist, subvert and regain their agency.

Just as Levada's career that was undermined by his ideological inclinations in the 1960s, Kozlova paid an academic price for her scholarly dedication to a more reflexive, empathy-driven quest for a grounded theory of the Soviet society. Her reliance on 'human documents', and their interpretation, her defence of empathic, participatory knowledge as 'a way of knowing' went against the mainstream positivist principles of producing sociological knowledge through surveys and other quantitative methods. Her methods were sometimes ridiculed and she wrote about this uphill battle with transparency and reflexivity, defending her methods and embedding her approach in the Western tradition of social theory and analysis.

The recognition of Kozlova's unique contribution to studying the Soviet past unfortunately came only after her untimely death in 2002. Over the past few years her colleagues at the Russian State University for the Humanities (RGGU) have organized a number of commemorative events and conferences that drew on her work and attempted to systematically discuss Kozlova's intellectual contribution and her original method of textual analysis focused on the human documents from the everyday life.

Kozlova's scholarship of Soviet society was transformational in a number of ways. It changed our scholarly views about what could be considered 'data'. Kozlova showed how meaningful a brief family postcard could be in social analysis and what individual text can teach us about social rules and norms. Challenging a positivist stance of trying to fit analytical models and classifications onto society, she demonstrated it is possible and necessary to understand Soviet individuals from the inside out. Such scholarly orientations as maintaining empathy and distance to the subject simultaneously, methodological reflexivity and self-awareness, respect for agency in the everyday life and the appreciation for social norms and constraints were all central to Kozlova's work.

Not fully recognized and appreciated in the 1990s and, at times, even today, Kozlova's work is more relevant now than ever.[1] The studies of Soviet society relying on post-classical sociology and post-positivist methodologies have proliferated over the last two decades, especially among historians and cultural theorists. A community of scholars is trailing the intellectual path Natalia Kozlova had started, sometimes without realizing her important legacy. In an atmosphere of fears about the renewed Cold War and the understandable focus on Russia's increasingly repressive political regime, Kozlova's intellectual legacy is even more pertinent. This legacy provides alternative ideas for studying social change (or stasis) in Russia that is not entirely dependent on the regime dynamics and that always involves social agency, interaction and creative invention.

Looking back through the embodied self: Natalia Kozlova's experimental quest for the Soviet Atlantis

Natalia Kozlova's research of the Soviet society developed during the 1990s along interdisciplinary lines. Starting out as a philosopher in the 1970s, by the 1990s she moved to studying the Soviet past relying on contemporary sociological theory. Grounded in historical materialism, Marxist-Leninist philosophy in the Soviet Union was analytically connected to real social relations and therefore close to sociology. Kozlova's work combined the concerns of classical sociology focused on issues of transition to modern society and the insights from post-classical sociological studies. She was particularly enthusiastic about the ideas of French sociologists such as Pierre Bourdieu, Paul Ricoeur, Michel de Certeau, Michel Foucault and Maurice Merleau-Ponty. Methodologically, Kozlova developed her inquiry following anthropological principles of research. Her studies of Soviet society had an applied character: she brought the sociological theories and ideas to make sense of the Soviet everyday life as it was seen and recorded by ordinary Soviet people. Theoretically, Kozlova argued for a 'grounded theory' – an approach to social analysis that keeps the observer attentive to the subject instead of transposing pre-developed analytical schemes and frames on the subjects of analysis.

Kozlova studied Soviet society through 'peoples' archives' – a collection of everyday documents created by ordinary individuals – diaries, postcards, letters, family photographs, memoirs and so on – what she called 'the meat' of history (Kozlova 2005: 11). 'Peoples archive' was a non-governmental organization founded in 1988 by the historians of the Moscow State Historical-Archival Institute. The founders sought to preserve the everyday documents of Soviet life, including personal and family archives, as well as archives of informal organizations (including the dissidents) and collections of letters and petitions sent by Soviet citizens to newspapers, journals and magazines.

Kozlova was very cognizant and analytical about her method and the potential biases she might be bringing into her study. Referring to herself as a 'test-subject observer' and deeply aware of her personal involvement, Kozlova saw her exploration, study and scholarly quest of understanding Soviet people to be very personal in nature:

> Every person carries his or her personal history in his body and language along with the history of the society. The general history I carry with me is for the most part Soviet. I see it as my duty to tell that history, while understanding that my voice is a voice of 'a once existing' [Soviet] person. Suffering through

the post-Soviet experience along with others, I simultaneously dive into the archeological layers of the soviet history. (11)

In the preface to her last book *The Soviet People: Scenes from History* (*Sovetskie liudi: Stseny iz istorii*), Kozlova reflected on her 'involved' reaction (she referred to it as ontological co-participation):

> After reading into these documents, you see the surroundings in a different light. What I see in the street, and my life today provides me with the frame for reading these documents (a 'reading position/stance'). I suddenly realized (not only by reading books) that method is not only a path; it is also a glance, and a feeling. (13) [. . .] What you read from a text is supported by the memory of your consciousness and your body. Body, like memory, is filled with the history that had happened. No body or language exist outside of society. (14) [. . .] If you lack constant reflection, a researcher can easily take up a position of an absolute observer, as if he/she is watching the social theater scene from the 'grand lodge', from the historically safe place. (15)

Such position of methodological reflexivity is usual for the field of anthropology, often critical of scientific methods in economics and political science that rely on positivist epistemology and a more radical break between the observer and the subject. Kozlova reflected on the intertwined nature of theory and the observer's own embodied experiences in a very accessible way:

> And then one's theoretical effort and the work of memory begin to stimulate each other, bringing an opportunity of a new analytical lens. Theoretical work turns into an autobiography of sorts. The stories of 'strangers' weave into your own. You get locked into a complex knot of reasons, the consequences of which you live through today. Your own unique individual life cannot be thought of outside the history of society. It is this history that makes your life unique. You see society as a zone from which you

> have emerged yourself. Your consciousness cannot delete the simplest, most banal self-evident truths. . . . They are mysterious by themselves and do not match your 'self' entirely. The content of the archives turns into an ordered system of meanings. (19)

Kozlova's methodology focused on interpreting the text and identifying that 'ordered system of meanings' to understand the Soviet society. She viewed language as a repository of sedimented social meanings. Through language an individual obtains an institutionalized programme for everyday life (47). Through language an individual and social 'common sense' is constructed and exercised. 'Social experience gets organized according to the norms of organizing meanings', Kozlova writes, which 'leads to the routinization of perceptions and objectification of practical action schemes' (Kozlova 2005: 45). Relying on Bourdieu concept of *habitus* – deeply engrained habits, norms and predispositions acquired through experience and socialization – Kozlova attempted to resolve the duality between an individual and society. 'Habitus is a sociality and history built into the language and the body of an individual', she claimed (73).

Every historical era has its collection of the dominant views, ideas and institutional models that guide our perceptions of what works and what does not. They develop as a result of earlier experiences, of the achievements and failures different nations go through, of the political choices made by the elites and the people. A deep faith in the superiority of Western civilization and Western institutional models coloured the first post-communist decade. Kozlova suggested that this Western-centric lens might explain why many scholars of their own culture sometimes take a position of the *judge* using the conceptual apparatus that developed in a different cultural system and claiming their right for intellectual and moral judgement (16).

> The West is a land of the miracles where the most cherished dreams of the former Soviet person come true. (16)

Kozlova resisted this Western orientation and viewed Soviet society as a civilization that needed to be studied on its own terms.[2]

The games people play in Soviet society

Following Norbert Elias, Pierre Bourdieu and other sociologists, Natalia Kozlova drew on game metaphor to interpret social action and interaction. This analogy of social action as comprising individual 'moves' in a game with particular rules and from a specific position is very different from, say, looking at social action as fulfilling a specific function within a social system. The latter perspective was associated, for example, with Talcott Parson's structural functionalism that was discussed earlier.

People's participation in games means that they recognize, accept and rely on the rules. Societies maintain themselves as long as social actors follow these rules. Rules do not mean that actors follow them literally. There are spaces and moments when actors make choices and can use or even manipulate the game in their own favour.[3] Actors are creative agents.

> The concept of 'the actor' makes people active. They are not toys hanging on the threads of the structures. They are not epiphenomenal to structures. Their actions [. . .] influence the outcomes of social change. [. . .] On the one hand, the term 'actor' relativizes our conceptions of a subject and, on the other hand, it leaves space for the diversity of forms and degrees of subjectivity. (61)

Kozlova explained that the advantage of the game metaphor is that it allows for avoiding the rigid binaries of individual versus society, freedom versus constraints, spontaneity versus determinism (65). It reveals the duality of these categories. It presents social process as a probabilistic process. Power in this analysis is not a category that is owned by some actors. Power is more about power relationships. There are no powerless. Everyone participates in the game thereby keeping it going. Understood this way, Soviet citizens could not be atomized or passive. Instead, they were active participants in making and remaking the Soviet society.

What type of information and observations can you extract about Soviet society and Soviet people when reading the written documents that reflect the everyday life in a society? Kozlova's approach postulated accessing the sphere of the social through specific individuals and through careful observation of the imprint of the social on the individual. Her archival research and close reading of people's documents produced insights into various periods of Soviet life and how social norms and concerns changed over time, into the symbolic resources that people relied on to develop meanings and stories of their lives, into the fateful events that changed lives' trajectories, and the everyday practices that might have differed depending on one's position in society. Her research was always presented through individual stories that made up the Soviet history. People, specific individuals, were central in her analysis. Let's look at some of these stories.

Kozlova's *The Soviet People: Scenes from History* includes the discussion of biographical notes of Vasily Ivanovich Vasil'ev (born in 1906), who started his narrative from 1917 (the year of Bolshevik Revolution) and told the story of his life, reflecting on his encounters with the terror of 1937, the Second World War and the post-war era. Focusing specifically on issues of pain and trauma, Kozlova carefully disentangles the different parts of his narrative. She notes the predominance of the passive voice in these memoirs: Vasil'ev did not see himself as an active subject. He simply lived in the whirlwind of history, surrendering to the forces moving things around him. Some of his memories are apparently traumatic: he recollects a story of being tied to the horse carriage to be able to run after it in order to survive the winter cold (because he did not have warm clothing) and obey the order given to him by his party superiors in (Kozlova 2005: 83–4).

Some of Vasil'ev's stories come close to mythologizing and combine elements of reality with fairy-tale-like elements. Kozlova is careful to point out parts of the narrative that include such elements as rationalizations as well as the use of cultural clichés, when the author relies on widely familiar narrative patterns that the Soviet citizens absorbed from movies and literature.

Kozlova notes the central role of psychological trauma and bodily pain in shaping Vasil'ev's memory, thereby highlighting that Stalinism left deep scars in the Soviet society. This careful attention to *embodied* history is central to Kozlova's approach. 'The memory of the mind and the body mutually support each other', she writes (106). 'We do not learn much about "facts" but, rather, "sense" different forms of perceiving and reconstruct conceptualizations' (105).

Another Soviet man featured in Kozlova's book is Ivan Ivanovich Belonosov. Born in 1908 Belonosov was from a peasant background and left extensive personal documents. He lost his father at the age of sixteen and later, his young wife (after marrying at nineteen). Both died from tuberculosis. Having graduated from pedagogical technical school, he studied history in college and became an archivist. He joined the Bolshevik party in 1940. The Second World War interfered with his education. He fought in the war and, upon his return, worked first at the Ministry of Foreign Affairs and then became the archivist at VTsSPS (All-Union Central Council of Trade Unions).

True to his profession, Belonosov kept an archive of his personal documents that includes his own biographical writings, a diary written over a long period of time as well as a variety of forms, cards, letters and souvenirs produced by state institutions. This treasure trove of different sources can help in the historical reconstruction not only of the everyday life but also of the genealogy of the social classification and categorization systems, argues Kozlova. She writes: 'The agents' position in the social field governs the ways specific social spaces are represented. We start understanding how Ivan Ivanovich obtained his "writing position" and his angle of seeing [. . .]' (140).

Belonosov's world view was structured by his early reading of the main Soviet propaganda textbook, *The Short Course on the History of the All-Union Communist Party* (*Kratky kurs istorii VKP(b)*) that was published in 1938. In his biographical writings Belonosov worked on developing a model Soviet story presenting his own life as a glorious, forward-looking path that took him from a simple peasant background, through education and the army, to a life of a diplomat. Just as the main Soviet textbook of the time presented a teleological view of history progressing from the traditional world to new, Soviet modernity, so too did Belonosov describe his own life. Belonosov's personal history appears to be very abstract and reduced to a particular model (Kozlova 2005: 123). An 'agent of a particular legitimation order', Belonosov's self-representation is constructed entirely in terms offered by the system (142). One could not find any gaps between the ways he described himself and his life and the dominant slogans, narratives and ideas advanced by the Soviet regime. Belonosov was an active contributor to the reproduction of the dominant social order through his archival work, his public dedication to Marxism-Leninism and his research and writings about the trade unions. Kozlova suggested that this work on maintaining and reproducing the social order required a lifelong commitment from Belonosov (142).

Unlike Vasil'ev's writings that gave away signs of pain and trauma inflicted on the author, Belonosov's writing appears to be void of any. 'It is anesthesia all-around', suggests Kozlova, who finds traces of pain only in Belonosov's last writings from the hospital, where he (aged 73) appears to suffer from loneliness (142). Kozlova suggests that Belonosov was continuing to write while he was working and felt 'as a part of the present and the emergent future'. He considered himself in the state of 'moral death' over the last twenty years of his life, when he stopped working. He passed away in 2000.

While some individuals in Kozlova's study (such as Belonosov) represented the 'model' Soviet people, whose angle of seeing and writing were produced by the Soviet discursive field, others were not. Not everyone in the Soviet Union lived and spoke the language of Soviet posters. There were exceptions. There were those, outside the Soviet game, who fell out the Soviet discursive matrix. One such unique example Kozlova explores is a life story of Evgenia Kiseleva, a simple woman from a small town in Ukraine, who directly experienced the war front, occupation and arduous post-war years marked by a dysfunctional second marriage to an alcoholic.

With only five years of schooling, Kiseleva was an unlikely person to pick up a pen and write the story of her life. Her world is rarely written about from the inside perspective. Most of such stories are told and could be collected as oral histories but they are not usually written down. Writing was not practised as a means of self-expression and self-representation in Kiseleva's surroundings. Her rare manuscript therefore provides a unique entry point into the worldview and the everyday life circumstances of someone otherwise often ignored. No wonder this particular manuscript has received extensive attention of scholars.[4]

Born in 1916, Kiseleva started writing late in life, at the age of sixty-four. A single retired woman (she divorced her second husband after twenty-one years of, what she presents as, very tortuous relationships), she found herself for the first time with some leisure time, an urban resident, watching TV and listening to the radio. Irina Sandomirskaia (a cultural theorist and Natalia Kozlova's academic collaborator) conjectured that Kiseleva must not have found herself in all the stories she watched on TV and listened to on the radio, and decided to write her own story. She wrote with a clear hope that she would find a reader. She wrote thinking that her life story could be turned into a movie. It is with this idea that in 1976 she sent her manuscript to the Gorky film studio in Moscow. Elena Olshanskaia, an editor working at the studio, saved the manuscript from the oblivion. Olshanskaia typed out the hand-written manuscript but was not able to find any publishers. The manuscript waited until 1991, when a few chapters were published in *Novyi Mir* and recognized as the journal's publication of the year. Natalia Kozlova found the original manuscript later, in the People's Archive, which had been established after the Soviet collapse to collect personal papers from individuals (Sandomirskaia 2012).

Unlike the diaries and biographical notes of many other Soviet people, Kiseleva's writing is not Soviet in style. It is a form of 'naïve writing' that is closer to traditional folklore and the forms of speaking in the lower strata of society. It does not follow strict grammatical and orthographical rules. But it does have its own patterns and style that, as observed by one historian, makes the narrative easily adaptable to a cinematic format (as was also intended by the author) (Paperno 2011).

Kiseleva's text allowed Kozlova to unearth different 'codes' and 'rules' governing the author's vision of life. Many of them are revealed through proverbs that reflect publicly accepted representations of practices, mental models of the world and attempts to explain actions (296). The text shows that Kiseleva abides by this obligatory code; it is part of the common sense people like her live by. It is the wisdom of the traditional world and the small community where people are closely tied to and depend on each other. It is the world where archaic and ritualistic actions, signs and superstitions are still an organic part of life. This world had co-existed with evolving Soviet realities. It also came into conflict with the new, modernizing trends. Kozlova suggests that Kiseleva's notes could also be seen as the history of the decomposing traditional values, norms and expectations as the conditions that allowed for their existence have changed. Unlike Belonosov (discussed earlier), whose peasant background did not interfere with his very Soviet life story of social mobility, Kiseleva was outside the 'big Soviet game' and never really adapted to the new social code. She still played the game contributing to the reproduction of the Soviet society. Without her participation (and of many others, like her), Kozlova argues, Soviet society would not have been possible.

In the second half of her life Kiseleva lives in the city, watches TV and listens to the radio. With that she enters a bigger world of Soviet political discourse. 'She "slept" through Stalin, but Brezhnev was a solid part of her life', notes Kozlova. Her city life is very different and her narrative constantly moves between 'then' and 'now'. It is this new life that makes Kiseleva's writing about her past possible and even imperative. After leaving her second husband (a radical break with her tradition), she learns to live alone, facing loneliness and the lack of a close community she is so used to. The peace and relative stability of the 1960s–1970s allows this simple woman to 'breathe out' through her writing that serves a therapeutic function, as she writes about her past – so dangerous, unstable and ever at the edge.

Kozlova emphasizes that Kiseleva's moral code and worldview are built around the value of survival. 'She does not face the question of "living in truth,"' Kozlova writes. 'Survival is the ultimate issue and value' (304). The manuscript refers to many close brushes with death Kiseleva had in her life. As a child, she experienced the threat of dying from cold, hunger and starvation. As a young wife and a mother, she lost her family happiness to war. On 22 June 1941 – the day the Wehrmacht invaded the USSR – she gave birth to her son. These two simultaneous events represent a personal watershed moment after which her life went downhill. Her war stories are dramatic and traumatic: she describes her encounters with the German army, while sitting in the trenches, with a little kid and a recently born baby.

Another story is of her mother dying from a shell exploding in her house at the moment when the family was in the basement and her mother went up for an errand. The post-war years are full of personal drama: her alcoholic husband left her and returned back over and over again. Tuberculosis, war, hunger and numerous family deaths: the issues of life and human mortality were the only constant in Kiseleva's life.

> Soviet peoples' notes are not simply the notes of the elderly who are not interested in the future [. . .]. These are the 'notes of those who survived the others.' Kiseleva's life experience tells us that any means that enable living are good. (308)

Soviet society changed after the Second World War. The late Soviet period – specifically the Brezhnev era – is often referred to as an era of stagnation. The dangers of dying from hunger, war or state terror were no longer central in shaping peoples' dispositions in life. The higher level of security Soviet people experienced during these years meant that their everyday lives changed along with the transformation of political and ideological structures. Lofty ideological goals promoted by the system in the 1920s and 1930s gradually shifted in the direction of emphasizing the private sphere and orienting the Soviet person towards finding happiness through personal relationships, love and friendship (Pinsky 2018). The boundaries of personal possibilities expanded along with the allowance for a Soviet person to be of a more humble type, make mistakes and be ordinary. The era of the 'superheroes' from the 1930s, who sacrificed themselves to achieve collective goals, had ended (Hooper 2008). The search for authenticity (*podlinnost'*), sincerity and contribution to the common, Soviet good was an individual choice that could be realized in exceptional places and circumstances such as the big developmental and construction projects in Siberia (Rojansky 2018).

Kozlova inquired into the years of stagnation and the new Soviet generation using the same methods she relied on to explore the everyday realities of the Stalinist era. One window into the everyday life of these post-war decades was provided through family correspondence. The family letters and postcards of Elena Petrovna M. (born 1933)[5] had accumulated over the period of 1972–90. They provided Kozlova with rich materials to explore the social changes that could be detected both through the new linguistic repertoire and the reflection of new behavioural practices in these documents.

The family letters carried an important social function, suggests Kozlova. They helped to maintain familial ties and create a sense of family, thereby recreating it as an aspect of social relations. They also provide a good glimpse into the everyday 'survival' practices during the late Soviet period. So what can we learn from such family correspondence? Food shortage is the first feature, Kozlova notes. The female members of the family (who were mostly responsible for procuring food in the shops) constantly note the quality of food supplies in the shops. Some complain about the absence of meat products; discuss the availability of dairy products and vegetables. These commentaries reveal the everyday concerns and life situations common to late Soviet existence. Shortages subside during elections. Various celebratory events (such as historical anniversaries in specific cities) can also help to fill the shops. Letters reveal everyday practices of coping and compensating for these shortages. Kozlova notes that contrary to widespread views of Soviet people as passive and paternalistic in their orientation to the state, this family correspondence shows the creativity and the entrepreneurial talents at play in ways Soviet people tried to compensate for the rigidities and inefficiencies of the Soviet economic system. 'Without such compensatory actions of social agents [. . .] this economy would not have survived', argues Kozlova (414).

The informal economy proved to be a big part of such compensatory activities. This correspondence makes it evident that Soviet people grew and canned their own food, knitted and sewed their own clothes and engaged in various types of informal exchanges. This informal economy was based on norms of mutual help and reciprocity. Older generations were giving. Younger generations were receiving.

With 80 per cent of the Soviet public having come from peasant background, Soviet people valued collectives they were part of. Kozlova notes that the late Soviet life brought out the importance of the working collectives. People projected family relations onto the working collectives: they valued their colleagues and maintained these relationships long after they might have left their jobs. Weddings, anniversaries and various types of personal celebrations always involved colleagues at work besides the family and the relatives.

Levada's surveys produced different results on the issue of Soviet collectivism. Levada's *Homo Sovieticus* was an atomized, lonely individual, exactly fitting the model developed by totalitarian theorists. Kozlova's Soviet person, by contrast, was embedded in and an integral part of the social surrounding. Contemporary memoirs and nostalgic ruminations about Soviet socializing in the kitchens, warm relationships with the neighbours and in the workplace probably better prop Kozlova's view on this issue. Many in Russia would emphasize today the alienating properties of the market-induced inequalities. But it is also undoubtedly true that the Soviet dominance over the social sphere did not allow for the formation of civic ties that would be autonomous of the state.

The emergence of the sphere of leisure activities was another sign of changing times in the late Soviet period. The younger generations increasingly revealed that they privileged leisure over work. Work was often something to complain about (420).

Contrary to the linguistic/discursive practices of the Stalinist era, the late Soviet person did not normally speak the language of Soviet posters. The official, ideological language was only used when people had to address official institutions (420). Even those who were professionally committed to the development and reproduction of the ideological discourse (such as Elena Petrovna's brother who taught scientific communism), in family correspondence, reveal concerns about private and material things such as borrowing money, paying taxes, along with a constant worry about how the weather affects one's health. Younger people showed distance towards the ideological language by integrating various terms and references in a more humoristic or ironic formats. They also retreated into the private world of personal hobbies, knitting, gardening and the like.

Kozlova, who read these letters in the middle of the 1990s, highlighted various elements of life that were taken for granted by late Soviet people. A Soviet person expected the stability of the ruble, regularity of salary and pension payments, the right for maternity leave, had hopes for free housing that, though not available immediately, was a sphere in which people tried various informal strategies. These self-evident truths of the Soviet everyday stood in a striking contrast to the realities of the 1990s, that Kozlova lived and worked in. She deemed these observations important for understanding the social realities in post-Soviet Russia. They provided an insight into the void experienced by the Soviet people when what they considered to be a norm had disappeared.

Conclusion

Academics often delight in rejecting the dominant and fashionable theories of their day. Yuri Levada was apparently ill-fit in the tight jacket of Marxism-Leninism and historical materialism propagated in the Soviet social sciences and found inspiration in the sociological approaches advanced in the 1950–1960s in the United States. By the late 1980s and early 1990s, when Levada was able to implement his ideas in empirical research, these ideas dominated the public space. The collapse of the Soviet Union represented a symbolic triumph of the Western ways of seeing the world.

Natalia Kozlova's scholarship also grew out of a sense of opposition. Feminist scholars have long highlighted the gendered nature of ideas advanced during the Cold War (Tickner 2005). The end of the Cold War became associated with greater pluralism in social and human sciences. Feminists and other critical theorists rejected positivist methodologies in favour of post-positivism, critical theory and, more historically contingent, interpretivist, linguistic and ethnographically based methodologies. The target of Kozlova's intellectual opposition was the totalitarian paradigm and the sense of Western triumphalism that negated the Soviet experience as a sui generis society that needs to be comprehended on its own terms.

The predominance of the totalitarian paradigm, according to Kozlova, foreclosed a more grounded exploration of Soviet social practices because it predetermined a simplified and politically driven interpretation of the Soviet person. Going against the grain of totalitarianism by highlighting the needs of individual adaptation and resistance to the repressive regime, Kozlova called for an alternative approach that would view Soviet society and its reproduction to result from multiple and fragmented actions of social agents who lived in the system and used it for their own purposes.

Such an approach – Kozlova argued – driven by a more grounded and non-ideological analytical lens, is better fit for understanding contemporary Russia. Her attention to the taken-for-granted elements of the Soviet reality helps comprehend the nature and extent of loss and trauma society underwent as a result of the abrupt transition. Kozlova's inquiry into these personal stories helps in understanding how the collective trauma of the 1990s turned into a big stumbling block used by the Russian leadership to avoid change (Sharafutdinova 2020).

CHAPTER 6
HOMO POST-SOVIETICUS AS A FIGHT FOR THE CONTINENT

No man is an island entire of itself; every man is a piece of the continent, a part of the main; if a clod be washed away by the sea, Europe is the less, as well as if a promontory were, as well as any manner of thy friends or of thine own were; any man's death diminishes me, because I am involved in mankind. And therefore never send to know for whom the bell tolls; it tolls for thee.

(John Donne)

The most common and pernicious connotation of *Homo Sovieticus* – as a passive, brainwashed individual who reveres authority and has no civic responsibility – is rooted in the politics and ideological clashes of the Cold War. Putin's leadership of Russia, which has culminated first in the annexation of Crimea and then moved on to a brutal war against Ukraine, has given many reasons for the resurrection of the term. Many symbols, practices and institutions from the Soviet era have experienced a comeback in Russia today. It is easy for observers to bring back the terms from the era long gone, too. Nonetheless, for most contemporary scholars in history, anthropology, psychology and cultural studies the term appears to be an *anachronism* of the Cold War. Soviet society and the Soviet system are radically different from contemporary Russian society and the political system that emerged under Putin. The Soviet flag returning to the streets on May 9th parades and more widely to Russian streets in 2022 symbolizes the nostalgic spasms of longing for the Soviet civilization. But they represent a reaction to the specific historical moment the Russian society finds itself in today: deeply unequal, divided and ruled by the kleptocratic elites who followed their delusions of greatness to the detriment of the country's future and its present.

Those in Russia who might still today believe in Russia's president are akin to that elderly woman with a red flag in Ukraine, who made headlines mistakenly thinking that the soldiers she sees in her village in April 2022 have come from Russia to liberate her. They are disoriented and willing to accept lies. They have fallen under the spell of a skilfully managed national identity politics that played with resentment and victimhood politics to mobilize support for the country's leader. The image of this woman has turned into a meme and has been since displayed through artwork in Ukraine's captured territories and inside Russia. The image is widely revered and associated with the official Russian patriotism. But does it have a future? Comparing this image to those widely circulated in Ukraine – of Ukrainian families and children who have lost their limbs and loved ones to this senseless war, whose future would you bet on?

The literal answer to this question is determined by the hard facts of biology and human lifespan. In an ironic twist of fate, this old woman with the Soviet flag is a fitting symbol of Putin's Russia today. It is only a matter of time that the Russian society will have to face openly the dead end of Putin's leadership driven by the sense of Russia's victimhood. The revenge imperative that the ageing Russia's leaders are enacting in Ukraine will only accelerate the political demise of the system erected over the past two decades. This deadly imperative is unsustainable.

Russia's future as a country today is deeply uncertain. Writing this last chapter of the book – about Russia's future – in the middle of Russia's aggressive war in Ukraine is filled with uneasiness. We do not know how long the war will still last. We have no means of knowing how exactly it will end. We do not know where the country's future boundaries will be. Nonetheless, there are things we do know. The changes that are ahead for post-war Russia would need new elites, new values, new collective identities and new ideas about what it means to be a citizen of Russia. These changes might not emerge immediately after war. They are likely to require more time. Just look at Ukraine. The post-Soviet Ukrainian society has been in active formation over the last two decades since at least the Orange Revolution in 2004. The societal dynamism and strength have been revealed through changing governments and leaders: over the past two decades Ukrainian citizens have elected five different presidents. Russia, on the other hand, had only one president since 2000 (especially, if we discount the brief interlude with Dmitry Medvedev's presidency during 2008-2012, who kept the presidential seat warm for Vladimir Putin).

So where do we look for these new ideas and identities that might be important for Russia's future? There is no other place but the Russian society. Even in Russia the Putin-style identity politics did not affect the whole of society. The images of Russia's returning greatness and national exceptionalism are important for many, but they are not important for all Russians. There is a significant age factor that differentiates those for whom other values and aspirations have become more important than the images of their country's greatness.

Historians such as Yuri Slezkine (2017) emphasized the role of books and literature in raising successive Soviet generations. Russia's youngsters today have different heroes. The rapid spread of new communication technologies and social media made the role of books and television marginal. Even in a country notorious for the love of books and reading, entertainment and infotainment are supplied today primarily by social media networks. The new media fosters new self-representations and new ways of relating to others. 'The app generation' growing up using social media platforms such as Facebook, YouTube, Instagram, Twitter, Tik-Tok and other applications is different from generations that crafted their lives and identities relying on different media.

Prior to Russia's war with Ukraine, this new generation had new celebrities and new social influencers. YouTube, for example, was a new source of celebrity culture in Russia and an important source of social influence. The new role models that emerged on YouTube lead their followers not only in making consumer choices but also in educating, motivating and inspiring them for action. Promulgating new social norms and values, they played a crucial role in the formation of individual identities. These new celebrity social influencers on various social media platforms have been the new source of cultural innovation and transmission. The Russian youth relied on modern video-bloggers to fill their quest for entertainment, learning and role models.

Social media influencers are normally viewed in the context of people's consumption patterns. Influencers are the new force in the world of marketing and advertisement and big retailers and brands increasingly rely on them to promote their products and services. While the appeal of social influencers to businesses is widely recognized, their influence on cultural change and identity formation of younger generations is less appreciated. But this influence may be even more important than their impact on consumption patterns. Young people today take their identity cues and develop self-representation strategies by following their media icons. The norms and values embedded in these media projects, and not only selected products advanced by influencers, help in forming new generations. These symbolic products – that is, the ideas of self – embedded in the advertising of specific products along with the video and ideational content created are much more important for producing the new person than the products themselves.

To take a selective look at these alternative forces that have shaped the Russian society before the war, in this concluding chapter I explore the identity cues supplied by Yuri Dud, a young journalist and a video-blogger who achieved fame and social influence through his YouTube programme *vDud*.[1]

The Russian digital space gave birth to a number of superstars, such as Olga Buzova and Anastasia Ivleeva, glamorous, self-made young celebrities followed by millions of young Russians. Following the successful examples of such global stars as Kim Kardashian and her mentor, Paris Hilton, they have promoted models of success in a capitalist society based on wealth and consumption. They have consciously stayed out of politics and their apolitical stance resonated with millions of Russians deeply distrustful of and disengaged from the political sphere. Yuri Dud was one of very few media icons and role models in Russia during the 2010s who has evolved in the direction of growing politicization and civic-ness.

Dud made his name as a sports magazine journalist. His real fame is based on his work as a YouTube video-blogger who reinvented the interview genre and made it keenly relevant and exciting to his audience. He also popularized the genre of documentary films producing several highly watched films on socially significant topics. His YouTube channel, *vDud*, was created in 2017 and had since developed followership of over eight million subscribers. The real social impact of his work is best illustrated by the after-effects of his documentary about HIV infection in Russia (Holt 2021). As reported by various media sources, the demand for express HIV testing kits has increased manifold after the broadcast of Dud's documentary on 11 February 2020.[2] Over thirteen million viewers watched the film within one week of its posting! (Holt 2021) No wonder, the online readers of *Forbes* magazine recognized Dud as the main cultural hero of 2020.[3]

Forbes magazine reported that in 2020 Yuri Dud was the most trusted Russian blogger and one of the most successful people under forty in Russia.[4] But where does Dud's influence come from? What elements of his programming and his presentation style and content appeal to his audience? What social norms and values does Dud transmit through his interviews and documentaries? Examining Dud's media project not simply as entertainment but in terms of the symbolic products and language advanced through his work can demonstrate the key necessary inputs into the process of formation of new, post-war Russian identities in the twenty-first century. It can also reveal the potential 'blind spots' – ideas and awareness that are needed for Russia's future but were not as clearly seen before the war.

These norms, ideas and values get revealed in Dud's project in various forms and contents. First, there are choices Dud makes in the process of selection of his interviewees and we can observe the evolution of this process in terms of its *trajectory*. The subjects of Dud's interviews reflect his view on what/who is 'hot' and what/who needs 'public attention'. Second, Dud makes choices of the questions he asks during the interview, thereby emphasizing certain topics, establishing norms of expected transparency and public openness on selected issues. Many of his questions are regular, so the audience gets exposed to discussions of, say, gender relations or salary size and sources of income over and over, becoming aware of the prevailing social norms, values and standards.

Third, Dud's long documentaries have emerged as an additional element of his media project and the topics selected and brought into the public discussion through these films are yet another important indicator of Dud's understanding of what is important and in need of public attention today. Dud's documentaries are turning into a significant educational and inspirational tool from which his followers learn about the country's history (recent and not so recent) and societal problems that require attention and collective and individual action. Dud's recent focus on individuals and organizations engaged in addressing these problems is particularly remarkable. His documentaries highlight the individual agency in organizing grassroots civic action that does not depend on the state. They raise hope by showing individuals and groups who bring positive change in Russia and inspire more of such activities.

Finally, Dud's media business model relies on advertisement, and Dud's ads can also be viewed as identity cues for a certain vision of the modern young self in Russia. These ads sell not only specific products, but the images of what it means to be a successful, modern and cool (*prodvinuty*) Russian today. The products advertised by Dud are, therefore, another window into identity production processes and into the new symbolic resources for Russia's new generations.

The choice of Yuri Dud might be questionable in the presence of even more famous digital celebrities with even larger audiences. However, Dud holds a special promise for Russia's future. He is in many ways similar to other digital celebrities in Russia in that he presents an image of a self-made man who relies only on himself and uses the opportunities of becoming rich and famous in the new digital era of capitalism. However, Dud has gone a step further by demonstrating and normalizing his active social and political stance. He has advanced an idea of Russian patriotism and hope for the country's better future with his interviews and documentaries that highlighted individual and collective action aimed at resolving important social problems in the country. He has presented an image of *Homo post-sovieticus* as a modern, successful and even 'cool dude' (no pun intended), who loves his country and is not afraid to raise difficult questions about its social and political problems. This socially responsible outlook that is presented in a way that is accessible and attractive to the new generations was an important trend that was growing in popularity in Russia. It is this trend that Russia would have to reinvent and rely on, if it is to have a future.

Symbolic products and identity goods
for the future Russian self

Dud's media production is quite extensive and is a testament to his work ethic and productivity. By January 2021, his work collection included 122 different video releases on YouTube most of which are interviews and 16 of which are documentaries. He has a team of experts helping him but he is the face behind the show.

The success and reinvention of the interview genre that Dud relied on was primarily due to the entertaining nature of *vDud* show. Dud invited celebrities from diverse spheres in life and asked very direct, personal questions in a relaxing, free-flowing context. He broke the ordinary rules of such interviews and asked questions about personal wealth, sources of earnings; about relationships, creative plans; likes and dislikes. Depending on who he interviewed, Dud could use swear words, along with his guests some of whom relied quite heavily on cuss language. Normally, his journalistic style allowed his interviewees to open up and show their humanity. This was also achieved by Dud being willing to travel to the places important to his interviewees. This was another important feature of his programme that allowed his audience to enter the lives of these individuals. Such mobility and travel to the personally significant physical spaces enhanced the opportunity for the viewer to empathize, understand the context and personally connect with the guest.

VDud show was more than entertainment. It informed and inspired. The informative aspect of the show has grown over time, as Dud started producing documentary films dedicated to selected topics. The show also worked to instil certain social norms and values. Dud could do that because he was in the position of symbolic power: he chose his guests, selected topics and questions, controlled the venue where his interviews were conducted and edited his interviews.

Dud's production reflected a very clear trajectory of moving from entertainment towards civic engagement. A journalist first created wide followership by connecting with the musical and other interests of younger generations in Russia, bringing in and talking frankly with famous rappers, rockers and other artists. The topics of his documentaries revealed his new interest in engaging with his followers on other issues – the important social issues in the country that are rarely discussed in an open fashion. His interviews revealed the nature of success in Russia, expanded on what is truly patriotic, and engaged with gender relations. His growing followership base reflected that the norms and values advanced through his programming resonated widely.

Dud left the country after Russia invaded Ukraine. In April 2022 Russia's government declared him 'foreign agent' adding his name to the growing list of foreign agent registry created in 2012. He continued his work and interviews abroad, openly discussing the war and the worsening political environment in Russia.

What is Russian success?

Yuri Dud himself represented a case of a modern-day success in Russia. Within a short time Dud became a popular vlogger with high earnings, mostly from advertisement. Given the rapidly expanding size of his YouTube audience, companies such as Eldorado, the largest retail chain of consumer electronics in Russia, made Dud their promo-agent. Dud also promoted other products and services, besides consumer electronics. Whatever he promoted, Dud did so drawing a very conscious linkage of the product to the specific image of the person he represented. This was the image of a young, modern, successful Russian citizen that is 'in business' (*v dele*).

'To be "in business" is not simply an advertisement campaign; it is also educational', Dud noted. 'We follow several basic principles in the advertisement. One of them is the imperative to share with your audience new knowledge and tell something interesting and useful' (Dud 2918).[5] 'To be in business' *a la* Dud you need to not only own a variety of digital gadgets but you need to use them to more fully develop your creative individual potential. In his more recent videos, Dud advertised applications for studying languages and for audio books, as well as services for buying airline tickets. Earlier, in 2017–2018 he participated in an advertisement campaign for Alfa bank and Head & Shoulders.

Based on his ads, Dud's vision of a successful *Homo post-sovieticus* was a modern individual who travelled a lot (and, of course, had money to travel), spoke different languages (and was therefore not parochial), took good care of him/herself (in terms of sports and personal hygiene), was at ease with technological progress and frugal (because he/she cared about various promotion-codes and ways of saving money).

Dud's choice of interviewees was another indicator of his notion of success. All the main heroes of Dud's interviews could be considered to be successful. Dud interviewed famous individuals who have pursued various ways of self-realization and self-actualization. Whether they were musicians, writers, politicians, photographers or stand-up comedians – their success was not measured by money only although the focus on income and earnings represented one of the signature traits in Dud's interview style. His question: 'how much do you earn' – has become a meme along with his question about Putin: "Is Putin a good guy?" (*Putin krasavchik?*). By going into the subject of earnings as well as how these earnings are made, Dud in effect showed to his audience how money could be made in Russia. These discussions were concerned with legitimate ways of earning and contained an important message that you do not need to be corrupt to be successful in material terms.

Dud's initial interviews in 2017–18 were mostly with musicians, singers and other video-bloggers who were very popular among different audiences in Russia. This first selection included specifically individuals well known for their intentionally shocking behaviour and *epatazh*. Whether it was Sergei Shnurov, a well-known leader of a band Leningrad, the rapper Basta or a video-blogger Amiran Sardarov famed for his blog 'A Diary of a Hach' (mocking Russians' prejudice towards Caucasians) – they all were famous individuals but, at the same time, not really through the conventional media channels such as television and radio. Hearing these conversations on radio or TV was probably not even possible given the amount of profanity used by many of Dud's heroes. Russia's Roskomnadzor, a governmental body overseeing online and media content fined Dud' for using profane language (*mat*). Dud' himself moved easily between different conversation styles, adapting to his interviewees.

Most of Dud's interviews were with Russians inside Russia but there were exceptions. Perhaps the biggest exception was his documentary about Russians in the Silicon Valley. The three-hour documentary titled 'How the world's IT capital works' aired in April 2020 and received much engagement as well as criticism. The focus on Russian entrepreneurs, often coming from outside Moscow, who were able to realize their dreams outside Russia was inspirational. Dud showed talented young Russians who wanted to change the world for the better and made money doing that. Following the release of this documentary, the main heroes were swamped by thousands of messages from young Russians who wanted to share their business ideas and wanted assistance in creating start-ups. Motivated and trying to respond constructively to such attention, Andrei Doronichev and Nikolai Davydov collaborated with Yana Belova and created an online community called 'Mesto' trying to recreate the spirit of the Silicon Valley in the virtual space.

The main ingredients of the individual success of most of Dud's heroes were found in the realm of self-realization through creativity and professional expertise that found the resonance and demand in society and economy (domestic and global). More recent documentaries extended these notions of success into the realm of civic orientation and commitment to taking action (however local) to address social problems.

Norms of individual civic-ness and patriotism

Dud's documentaries have turned into important educational projects that were motivated by civic values and patriotism. The choice of topics for these films had indicated that Dud moved beyond his initial focus on celebrities and found a new purpose, more civic and socially oriented, than his initial interviews. The documentaries have raised important social issues from different arenas such as the country's painful historical memory, degradation of Russia's Far East, public health and AIDS problem, social challenges and opportunities for action in Russia's provinces and other issues. These documentaries made it clear that Dud was a Russian patriot and the version of patriotism he promoted was very different from the patriotism promoted by the Kremlin.

Russian observers have long noticed that the patriotic education of youth had been at the centre of the Kremlin's ideological agenda (Laruelle 2015; Goode 2017; Omelchenko et al. 2015). The Russian government has sought to activate patriotism through mobilizing historical symbols, such as that of the Soviet victory in the Second World War as well as earlier, pre-Soviet symbols that help to highlight to continuity of the Russian state. Such public ceremonies as Victory Day celebrations and educational projects that integrated patriotism teaching in school are all part of that agenda. In 2016, Russia's president referred to patriotism as 'our main national idea'.[6]

Dud provided young Russians with a different model of patriotism than the 'ura-patriotism' model that was promoted by the Kremlin. As a successful blogger who focused on Russian cultural products, individuals and history, he promoted an understanding that there are 'cool' people, things and activities in Russia. Dud's and his heroes' material and creative successes demonstrated to the audience that both of these things were achievable in Russia and that there was no need to leave the country.

Dud-style patriotism was autonomous from the Kremlin-led narratives and showed the young Russians that you do not have to show your love for the government to love your country. One of his guests, Mikhail Kozyrev, a well-known musical producer, mentioned, as his favourite line, words from a song by a young Russian rapper, FACE (Ivan Dremin): 'I love my country and I hate the state'. Many of Dud's interviewees were from creative professions and were opposed to the Kremlin and its policies.

Dud rarely interviewed people closely linked to the state and to the regime and mostly brought to his program people who were not given access to television. The fact that he did also invite such individuals as Dmitry Kiselev, Vladimir Zhirinovsky and Andrei Kolesnikov – who were closely aligned with the Kremlin's politics – underlined Dud's general principle of openness towards political differences – although some observers might argue that Dud invited them to 'crack them open' and show their 'guts'. Indeed, the journalist's professional intention is to open up the other person to the audience. What a person tries to hide – such as the compromises made with one's conscience – could presumably be revealed in the interview. But generally, as a good journalist, Dud did not promote any specific political agenda of his own and allowed his interlocutors to speak for themselves. His political preferences were not hidden far. It was quite clear that he supported accountable, democratic government and liberal values that placed him against the current regime in Russia.

The interview with Dmitry Kiselev, the Kremlin's chief pro-pagandist, was probably the hardest one for Dud. Kiselev, a skilful journalist himself, simply stonewalled Dud giving him long-winded and boring answers and requesting that the interview to be uncut and unedited. Critics suggested Dud lost that 'fight'.

Another patriotism-evoking feature of Dud's program was his attempt to show Russia and Russians outside the capital city of Moscow. Dud travelled with his guests to show the everyday life and engagements of his interviewees. Such immersion into the living and working environment of his guests was an important and very special feature of *vDud* show. The journalist practically invited his audience for a journey towards understanding the life goals, values and aspirations of his interviewees. The *immersion* mechanism made that process quite organic allowing the audience to live through those new worlds along with Dud.

One of the good examples of the power of such an approach was Dud's recent interview with Dmitry Markov, a famous photographer and a social worker who captured the everyday life images of people and places in Russia that got rarely exposed. Markov himself is a troubled personality with whom many Russians could probably associate. A former drug addict, he grew up in an orphanage and developed an interest in photography as the only thing that keeps him out of trouble. With a very deep sense of humanity, Markov exposed all his personal problems and vulnerabilities. At one point in the interview, he brought Dud to his rehab centre, where he goes to fight his demons.

The symbolic content of Dud's documentary about Markov was deeply humanist. Markov showed Dud his involvement with and help to two grassroots charity organizations in Kostroma and Pskov regions. The organization 'Rostok' helps young people and kids with mental disabilities to develop social and physical skills in a carpentry workshop where kids are taught to make various objects that are then sold. Another organization Markov talked about was lodging for the homeless, 'Resurrection'. It is another charity organization that helped people who lost their homes (usually due to drunkenness, mental issues or other social problems). This documentary had immediate resonance with the viewers. Markov informed later that within 24 hours after the release of this interview the two aforementioned charity organizations received 3 million rubles in donations.

Another of such documentaries was about a non-profit organization *Kruzhok*. In many ways, this documentary carried very similar messages. It highlighted the work of a group of successful Russian programmers who undertook a social project of inspiring and teaching teenagers in Russia's remote villages where opportunities for such learning were non-existent. The main symbolic message in this documentary was about the civic responsibility of those Russians who have made it individually in terms of their professional careers and material well-being.

These documentaries were instilled with patriotic feelings in other ways as well. The films captured and portrayed to viewers the natural and human beauty present in Russia. The incredibly beautiful natural landscapes of the Russian provinces were incorporated along with an intimate look at the Russian people: very imperfect in many ways and yet very human, relatable and lovable.

On knowledge and understanding

This book started with Daniel Kahneman's notion of slow and fast thinking. I want to end it with the advocacy for slow and grounded thinking, when it comes to building knowledge and understanding of the people and environments we are not part of.

In a recent article in *Nature* Darya Tsymbalyuk, a sociocultural anthropologist from Ukraine, a country in the midst of an aggressive military attack from Russia, wrote about the importance of embodied knowledge and its lacking place in the mainstream field of academic knowledge production. 'Our bodies are vessels of knowledge. [. . .] different bodies carry different memories and different perceptions'.

The anti-communist dissidents from Eastern Europe and Russia that I discussed in this book carried their knowledge of the communist system in their bodies, too. Their knowledge was undoubtedly instructed by their emotions of fear and anxiety, trauma and loss experienced over the course of the calamitous twentieth century. Yuri Levada carried his own knowledge of living in the Soviet Union, informed by personal professional career and personal intellectual strivings. The concept of *Homo Sovieticus* they helped to coin reflected that knowledge and experience that they processed through their thinking.

Natalia Kozlova also wrote about the importance of embodied knowledge in her exploration of the Soviet society. The main difference in her stance was that she was aware of this importance and she relied on it as a methodological tool for understanding individual experiences in the documents she studied. In some ways, Yuri Dud, a journalist and video-blogger, is akin to Natalia Kozlova, the sociocultural anthropologist, who used her own embodied experiences of living in the Soviet Union to understand Soviet people through their private letters, diaries and postcards. Only in Dud's case, he takes himself and his viewers into a multifaceted journey into the lives of contemporary Russians (albeit carefully selected ones) to impart his embodied knowledge about the diversity of human experiences in Russia today that might provide hope for Russia's future.

The important thing to remember is that in neither of the cases discussed in this book is the knowledge neutral and dispassionate as the mainstream social sciences expect it to be. Such realization should help us pause and be selective with the terms we use and be reflexive about the judgements we make about others, whose life experiences and perceptions might be very different from our own.

It is impossible to call for compassion to the Russians in the midst of an aggressive war fought on their name. Wars split and polarize. Wars create mortal enemies. Most importantly, wars dehumanize. The only response from the outside observers however should be focused on maintaining that humanity. Out ideas and perceptions shape the realities we live in. Ideas about people, particularly those that depict societies and groups as monoliths and that have long outlived whatever usefulness they once had, matter. Rethinking *Homo Sovieticus* today means recognizing the universality of our human condition and the constancy of human agency. Even while systems, structures and institutions might shape human agency, individuals are creative agents. Their actions can work to maintain those structures or to overcome and change them. Keeping up this faith in human agency and human capital in Russia is the only pathway, if we are at all to give a chance to the future of Russia.

NOTES

Prologue

1. Turkova (2021).
2. Borenstein (2019).
3. Fukuyama (2017).
4. Graham (2015).
5. 'Nuland Shares Concerns', 7 December 2021, https://www.tellerreport
   .com/news/2021-12-07-nuland-shares-concerns-about-putin-s-attempts
   -to-recreate-the-soviet-union.S15Lc1daYY.html
6. Nemtsova (2019).
7. Lozovsky (2015).
8. Bershidsky (2021).

Chapter 1

1. For example, see Tyszka (2009).
2. Shiller, Korobov and Boycko (1992).
3. https://lenta.ru/articles/2016/04/06/soviet_man/.
4. https://www.themoscowtimes.com/2017/10/13/the-evolution-of-homo
   -sovieticus-to-putins-man-a59189.
5. https://www.sakharov-center.ru/article/transkript-lekcii-daniila
   -dondurea-reinkarnacia-sovetskogo-celoveka; https://www.sakharov
   -center.ru/article/transkript-lekcii-daniila-dondurea-reinkarnacia
   -sovetskogo-celoveka.
6. Andrei Arkhangelsky, 'Mining konflikta i katastrophy: Chem putinskii
   chelovek otlichaetsia ot sovetskogo', https://carnegie.ru/commentary
   /75408.
7. https://lenta.ru/news/2021/10/21/homosoveticus/.

Notes

8. See also Ganev's (2017).

9. Irina Prokhorova, 'Mozhno zakryt' granitsy, no zapretit' dumat' nevozmozhno', *Skazhi Gordeevoi*, https://www.youtube.com/watch?v =rTwrrqwa0f4.

10. Fadeeva (2012).

Chapter 2

1. Yurchak (2005).

2. Barańczak (1990: 178).

3. Mazurska 2013: 94, from Miłosz, *Rozmowy polskie*, 544.

4. Barańczak (1990: 181).

5. Markov, *The Truth That Killed*, 182.

6. Warner (2014: 79).

7. Warner (2014: 85).

8. Warner (2014: 86).

Chapter 3

1. https://tass.ru/obschestvo/12558461.

2. Tolstoi and Gavrilov (2018).

3. 'Zinoviev to Yeltsin in 1990: "The West Applauds You for Destroying Our Country"' http://zinoviev.info/wps/archives/1339.

4. Lescaze (1978).

5. Tolstoi and Gavrilov (2018).

6. Borenstein, Homo Sucker, https://jordanrussiacenter.org/news/homo -sucker-russias-alien-nations.

7. This exchange produced a folk ditty about this famous exchange: 'Обменяли хулигана на Луиса Корвалана, где б найти такую б . . . ь, чтоб на Брежнева сменять?'

8. И так все – от членов политбюро, академиков и писателей до рабочих и колхозников – находят свое оправдание. Причем чаще всего люди искренне верят, что это их подлинные чувства.

Редко кто сознает, что это лишь отговорка, самооправдание. И уж совсем мало кто открыто и честно признается, что просто боится репрессий. Всего один за всю мою жизнь сказал мне, что его устраивает коммунистическое государство: оно позволяет ему зарабатывать деньги, печатая всякую демагогическую чушь в газетах.

9. Остальные же – хотят они этого или не хотят – строят коммунизм. Государству наплевать, какими теориями они оправдывают свое участие в этом строительстве, что они думают и что чувствуют. До тех пор пока они не сопротивляются, не протестуют и не высказывают публично несогласия, они устраивают советское государство. Любви никто не требует, все просто и цинично: хочешь новую квартиру – выступи на собрании; хочешь получать на 20–30 рублей больше, занимать руководящий пост – вступай в партию; не хочешь лишиться определенных благ, нажить неприятности – голосуй на собраниях, работай и молчи. Все так делают – кому охота плевать против ветра? На том и стоит это государство, продолжает морить людей по тюрьмам, держать всех в страхе, порабощать другие народы, угрожать всему миру.

Chapter 4

1. Most famously, the 1937 Soviet census results were not published and made secret because they revealed the extent of human loss in Holodomor. The state officials responsible for organizing the census were repressed.

2. For more on the history of Moscow-Tartu School, see Waldstein (2008).

3. Daria Dimke, who asked a similar question about the existence of academic classics without their classical works and academic texts, gave a similar answer. She pointed to the institutional context of the Soviet Union when 'speaking truth to power' and the mass audience were more important than theoretical discussions (Dimke 2012).

4. Dialectical materialism was a core element of Soviet political ideology.

5. https://www.business-gazeta.ru/article/399709.

6. This argument was first made by Gerschenkron (1962).

7. Brooks (2000: xv).

8. Arendt (1951).

9. In September 2016 the Levada Center was included in the registry of organizations acting as foreign agents in Russia.

10. Nichols (2022).

Chapter 5

1. A recent edited volume, *After Stalin: Late Soviet Subjectivity (1953-1985),* an impressive collection published in 2018, fails to mention Natalia Kozlova's work in the list of studies on Soviet subjectivity provided at the end of the book, for example.

2. In this approach, she built on the historian Stephen Kotkin's *Magnetic Mountain: Stalinism as a Civilization* (1995).

3. Note the difference of game metaphor in social theory from 'game theory' in economics that is based on stricter assumptions about rationality and rational behavior of actors, enabling a more rigid set of outcomes from the pre-determined game structure.

4. Besides Kozlova, other scholars engaged with Kiseleva's writings. For the most recent, see Paperno (2011).

5. The name has been changed.

Chapter 6

1. The name plays on Dud's last name and the Russian slang for 'having sex'/*vdut*.

2. https://www.vedomosti.ru/technology/articles/2020/02/17/823253-film -dudya.

3. https://www.forbes.ru/forbeslife/416225-yuriy-dud-stal-geroem-goda-po -versii-chitateley-forbes-life.

4. https://www.forbes.ru/profile/365143-yuriy-dud.

5. https://adindex.ru/news/creative/2018/08/15/173540.phtml.

6. https://www.rbc.ru/politics/03/02/2016/56b1f8a79a7947060162a5a7.

BIBLIOGRAPHY

Abuladze, Tengiz. (1986). *Pokaianie.* (film).

Adorno, Theodor, E. Frenkel-Brenswik, D. J. Levinson and R. M. Sanford. (2019). *The Authoritarian Personality.* New York: Verso Books.

Aksyonov, Vasily. (1987). *In Search of Melancholy Baby.* Trans. Antonina Bouis. New York: Random House.

Aleksievich, Svetlana. (2016). *Vremya sekond khend (Second-Hand Time).* Moscow: Vremya.

Alexievich, Svetlana. (2006). *Voices from Chernobyl: The Oral History of a Nuclear Disaster.* Trans. and with a preface by Keith Gessen. New York: Picador.

Alexievich, Svetlana. (2017). *The Unwomanly Face of War: An Oral History of Women in World War II.* New York: Random House.

Alexievich, Svetlana and Svetlana Aleksievich (1992). *Zinky Boys: Soviet Voices from the Afghanistan War.* New York: W. W. Norton & Company.

Applebaum, Anne (2012). *Iron Curtain: The Crushing of Eastern Europe, 1944–1956.* New York: Doubleday.

Arendt, Hanna. (1951). *The Origins of Totalitarianism.* New York: Schocken.

Arendt, H. (1973). *The Origins of Totalitarianism.* New York: Harcourt Brace Jovanovich.

Barańczak, Stanislaw (1990). *Breathing Under Water and Other East European Essays.* Cambridge, MA: Harvard University Press.

Bershidsky, Leonid. (2021). 'Thirty Years Gone, the Soviet Union Is Not Quite Dead'. 23 December 2021. https://www.bloomberg.com/opinion/articles/2021-12-23/the-soviet-union-may-have-imploded-30-years-ago-but-it-s-not-dead

Bikbov, Alexandr. (2014). *Grammatika poryadka: Istoricheskaya sociologiya ponyatij, kotorye menyayut nashu real'nost'[The Grammar of the Order: Historical Sociology of the Concepts that Change Our Reality].* Moscow: Higher School of Economics printing house.

Bikbov, Aleksandr and Stanislav Gavrilenko. (2003). 'Rossiskaia sotsiologiia: avtonomiia pod voprosom'. *Logos* 2 (37): 51–85.

Breslauer, George W. (1978). 'On the Adaptability of Soviet Welfare-State Authoritarianism'. *Soviet Society and the Communist Party*: 3–25.

Brooks, Jeffrey. (2000). *Thank You, Comrade Stalin! Soviet Public Pulture from Revolution to Cold War.* Princeton: Princeton University Press.

Bibliography

Bukovsky, Vladimir. (2007). *I vozvrashchaetsia veter*. Moscow: Zakharov.

Bykov, Dmitry. (2021). 'SSSR – strana kotoruiu pridumal Gaidar'. http://gaidarfund.ru/articles/1154/

Chatterjee, Choi and Karen Petrone. (2008). 'Models of Selfhood and Subjectivity: The Soviet Case in Historical Perspective'. *Slavic Review* 67 (4): 967–86.

Coleman, Heather J. (2017). 'Svetlana Aleksievich: The Writer and Her Times'. *Canadian Slavonic Studies* 59 (3-4): 193–5.

Dame, Natalia. (2019). 'Why is Sharikov Dead? The Fate of "The Soviet Frankenstein" in Bulgakov's A Dog's Heart'. *Canadian Slavonic Papers* 61 (1): 25–56.

David-Fox, Michael. (2011). *Showcasing the Great Experiment: Cultural Diplomacy and Western Visitors to the Soviet Union, 1921–1941*. New York: Oxford University Press.

Dimke, D. (2012). 'Classics without Classics: Social and Cultural Origins of Soviet Sociology Style'. *Sociological Studies (Socis)* 6: 97–106. — in Russ.

Dostoevsky, Fyodor. (1994). *Demons*. Trans. Roichard Pevear and La. Vintage Classic.

Dubin, B. (2007). 'Tradition, Culture and Game in Sociology of Yuri Levada'. *Social Sciences and Contemporary World* 6: 31–8. — in Russ.

Dubin, B. (2010). 'Late Soviet Society in Sociological Working of Yuri Levada in 1970s'. *Social Sciences and Contemporary World* 5: 101–10. — in Russ.

Edele, Mark. (2007). 'Soviet Society, Social Structure, and Everyday Life: Major Frameworks Reconsidered'. *Kritika: Explorations in Russian and Eurasian History* 8 (2): 349–73.

Ėtkind, Aleksandr. (2005). 'Soviet Subjectivity: Torture for the Sake of Salvation?'. *Kritika: Explorations in Russian and Eurasian History* 6 (1): 171–86.

Fadeeva, Liubov. (2012). *Kto my? Intelligentsiiq v borbe za identichnost*. Novyi khronograf.

Fanailova, Elena. (2011). 'Evropa v reshaiushchie momenty istorii. Milosh i sovremennost'. https://www.svoboda.org/a/24341453.html

Fedor, Julie and Rolf Fredheim. (2017). '"We Need More Clips About Putin, and Lots of Them:" Russia's State-Commissioned Online Visual Culture'. *Nationalities Papers* 45 (2): 161–81.

Firsov, B. M. (2012). 'Kak navodilis' mosty mezhdu sovetskoi I zarubezhnoi sotsiologiei, ili self-made sociologists'. In *Istoriia sovetkoi sotsiologii: 1950–80ee gg. Uchebnoe posobie*, 248–91. St. Petersburg: EUSPb Press.

Fitzpatrick, Sheila. (2002). *The Commissariat of Enlightenment: Soviet Organization of Education and the Arts under Lunacharsky, October 1917–1921*. Vol. 2. Cambridge: Cambridge University Press.

Franaszek, Andrzej. (2011). *Miłosz. A Biography*. Cambridge, MA: Harvard University Press.

Friedrich, Carl Joachim and Zbigniew Kazimier Brzezinski. (1956). *Totalitarian Dictatorship and Autocracy*. New York: Praeger.

Fritzsche, Peter and Jochen Hellbeck. (2009). 'The New Man in Stalinist Russia and Nazi Germany', in *Beyond Totalitarianism: Stalinism and Nazism Compared*, ed. by Michael Geyer and Sheila Fitzpatrick, 322. New York: Cambridge University Press.

Fukuyama, Francis. (2017). 'In Masha Gessen's "The Future Is History," Homo Sovieticus Rises'. *New York Times*, 3 October 2017. https://www .nytimes.com/2017/10/03/books/review/masha-gessen-the-future-is -history.html.

Gabowitsch, M. (2008). 'To The Discussion on Theoretical Legacy of Yuri Levada'. *Russian Public Opinion Herald* 4: 50–61. — in Russ.

Ganev, Venelin. (2017). 'The Spectre of Homo Post-Sovieticus'. *New Eastern Europe* 19 (10). http://neweasterneurope.eu/2017/10/19/spectre-homo -post-sovieticus/

Gerschenkron, Alexander. (1962). 'Economic Backwardness in Historical Perspective (1962)'. *The Political Economy Reader: Markets as Institutions*: 211–28.

Gessen, Masha. (2017). *The Future is History: How Totalitarianism Reclaimed Russia*. London, UK: Granta Books.

Geyer, Michael and Sheila Fitzpatrick. (2009). *Beyond Totalitarianism: Stalinism and Nazism Compared*. Cambridge: Cambridge University Press.

Goode, J. Paul. (2017). 'Humming Along: Public and Private Patriotism in Putin's Russia'. In *Everyday Nationhood*, ed. by Michael Skey and Antonsich, 121–46. Basingstoke: Palgrave Macmillan.

Graham, Thomas. (2015). 'Europe's Problem is with Russia, Not Putin'. *Financial Times*, 31 May 2015. https://www.ft.com/content/f0ff7324-03b5 -11e5-a70f-00144feabdc0

Гудков, Л. (2007). 'Советский человек» в социологии Юрия Левады'. *Общественные науки и современность* 6: 16–30.

Gudkov, Lev. (2001a). '"Totalitarizm" kak teoreticheskaia ramka: popytki revizii spornogo poniatiia'. *Monitoring Obshchestvennogo Mneniia* 5 (56): 20–9.

Gudkov, Lev. (2001b). '"Totalitarizm" kak teoreticheskaia ramka: popytki revizii spornogo poniatiia'. *Monitoring Obshchestvennogo Mneniia* 6 (56): 13–30.

Gudkov, Lev. (2004). '*Negativnaya udentichnost': Stat'i 1997–2002 godov*. Москва: Новое литературное обозрение.

Gudkov, Lev. (2005). '"Память" о войне и массовая идентичность россиян'. *Неприкосновенный запас* 2–3: 40–1.

Gudkov, Lev. (2007). 'Soviet Man'. *Yuri Levada's Sociology. Social Sciences and Contemporary World* 6: 16–30. — in Russ.

Gudkov, Lev. (2009). 'Usloviia vosproizvodstva sovetskogo cheloveka'. *Vestnik obshchestvennogo mneniia* 2 (100, April–June): 8–37.

Gudkov, L. D. (2008a). '"Soviet Man" in the Sociology of Iurii Levada'. *Sociological Research* 47 (6): 6–28.

Gudkov, L. (2008b). 'Limited Sanity Society'. *Russian Public Opinion Herald* 1: 8–32. — in Russ.

Hanson, Philip. (1988). 'Alexander Zinoviev on Stalinism: Some Observations on the Flight of Our Youth'. *Soviet Studies* 40 (1): 125–35.

Hanson, Philip and Michael Kirkwood. (1988). *Alexander Zinoviev as Writer and Thinker*. London: Palgrave Macmillan.

Hellbeck, Jochen. (2009). *Revolution on My Mind: Writing a Diary under Stalin*. Cambridge, MA: Harvard University Press.

Holt, Ed. (2021). 'Educating Russia about HIV/AIDS'. *The Lancet HIV* 8 (2): e66.

Hooper, Cynthia. (2008). 'Novomu sovetskomu cheloveku' sluchaetsia oshibatsia'. In Anatoly Pinsky (ed.), *Posle Stalina: Pozdnesovetskaia sub'ektivnost*, 39–74. St Petersburg: EUSPb Press.

Huang, Christine and Jeremiah Cha. (2020). 'Russia and Putin Receive Low Ratings Globally'. 7 February 2020. https://www.pewresearch.org/fact-tank/2020/02/07/russia-and-putin-receive-low-ratings-globally/

Kaganovsky, Lilya. (2008). *How the Soviet Man was Unmade: Cultural Fantasy and Male Subjectivity under Stalin*. Pittsburgh: University of Pittsburgh Press.

Kahneman, Daniel. (2011). *Thinking, Fast and Slow*. New York: Macmillan.

Karkov, Nikolay. (2018). 'Against the Double Erasure: Georgi Markov's Contribution to the Communist Hypothesis'. *Slavic Review* 77 (1): 151–73.

Kharkhordin, Oleg. (1999). *The Collective and the Individual in Russia: A Study of Practices*. Vol. 32. Berkeley: University of California Press.

Klumbytė, Neringa and Gulnaz Sharafutdinova, eds. (2012). *Soviet Society in the Era of Late Socialism, 1964–1985*. Lanham, MD: Rowman & Littlefield.

Koenker, Diane P. (2013). *Club Red: Vacation Travel and the Soviet Dream*. Ithaca: Cornell University Press.

Kozlov, Denis. (2013). *The Readers of Novyi Mir*. Cambridge, MA: Harvard University Press.

Kozlova, Natalia. (2000). 'Opyt sotsiologicheskogo chteniia "chelovecheskikh dokumentov" ili razmyshleniia o znachimosti metodologicheskoi refleksii'. *Sotsiologicheskie issledovaniia*, 9: 22–31.

Kozlova, Natalia. (2005). '*Sovetskie lyudi: Stseny iz istorii [Soviet People: Scenes from history].* Moscow: Evropa.

Kozlova, Natalia and Irina Sandomirskaya. (1996). "Ya tak khochu nazvat kino": Naivnoe pismo: opyt lingvo-sotsiologicheskogo chtenia". Russkoe fenomenologicheskoe obshchestvo: Gnozis.

Козлова, Н. Н. (1996). 'Горизонты повседневности советской эпохи: голоса из хора'. Москва: Институт филосифии РАН, 1-216.

Kravchenko, Artem. 'Sozdanie novogo sovetskogo cheloveka'. https://arzamas.academy/materials/1499

Krylova, Anna. (2000). 'The Tenacious Liberal Subject in Soviet Studies'. *Kritika: Explorations in Russian and Eurasian History* 1 (1): 119–46.

Laruelle, Marlene. (2015). 'Patriotic Youth Clubs in Russia. Professional Niches, Cultural Capital and Narratives of Social Engagement'. *Europe-Asia Studies* 67 (1): 8–27.

Laursen, Eric. (2007). 'Bad Words Are Not Allowed!: Language and Transformation in Mikhail Bulgakov's "Heart of a Dog"'. *The Slavic and East European Journal* 51 (3): 491–513.

Lescaze, Lee. (1978). 'Solzhenitsyn Says West Is Failing as Model for World'. *Washington Post*, 9 June 1978. https://www.washingtonpost.com/archive/politics/1978/06/09/solzhenitsyn-says-west-is-failing-as-model-for-world/

Levada, Yuri. (2001). 'Homo Praevaricatus: Russian Doublethink'. In *Contemporary Russian Politics: A Reader*, 312–22. Oxford: Oxford University Press.

Levada, Yuri. (2003). 'Sovremennost' Oruella: analogii i analiz'. *Vestnik obshchestvennogo mneniia*, 2003. http://ecsocman.hse.ru/text/18936622/.

Levada, Yuri. (2004). 'Chelovek sovetskii'. *Public Lecture*, 15 April 2004. https://polit.ru/article/2004/04/15/levada/

Levada, Yuri. (2006). 'Nauchnaia zhizn' – byla seminarskaia zhizn'. *Sotsiologicheskoe obozrenie* 5 (1): 114–20.

Levada, Yuri A. (1993). *Sovetskii prostoi chelovek*. Moscow: Intertsentr.

Lozovsky, Ilya. (2015). 'I'm a Russian-Born American Jew. My People's Rejection of Syrian Refugees Breaks My Heart'. 23 November 2015. https://www.washingtonpost.com/posteverything/wp/2015/11/23/im-a-russian-born-american-jew-im-heartbroken-that-my-people-have-so-little-sympathy-for-syrian-refugees/

Markov, Georgy. (1984). *The Truth That Killed*. Boston: Ticknor and Fields.

Mazurska, Joanna. (2013). 'Making Sense of Czeslaw Miłosz: A Poet's Formative Dialogue with His Transnational Audiences'. PhD diss., Vanderbilt University.

Mickiewicz, Ellen Propper. (1990). *Split Signals: Television and Politics in the Soviet Union*. New York: Oxford University Press on Demand.

Bibliography

Nemtsova, Anna. (2019). 'Russia's Twin Nostalgias'. *The Atlantic*, 7 Deecember 2019. https://www.theatlantic.com/international/archive/2019/12/vladimir-putin-russia-nostalgia-soviet-union/603079/

Nichols, Tom. (2022). 'Only Putin Knows What Happens Next'. *The Atlantic*, 23 January 2022. https://www.theatlantic.com/ideas/archive/2022/01/putin-knows-what-happens-next-ukraine/621348/

Omelchenko, Daria, et al. (2015). 'Patriotic Education and Civic Culture of Youth in Russia: Sociological Perspective'. *Procedia-Social and Behavioral Sciences* 190: 364–71.

Oushakine, Serguei Alex. (2003). 'Crimes of Substitution: Detection in Late Soviet Society'. *Public Culture* 15 (3): 427–51.

Oushakine, Serguei Alex. (2004). 'The Flexible and the Pliant: Disturbed Organisms of Soviet Modernity'. *Cultural Anthropology* 19 (3): 392–428.

Oushakine, Serguei Alex. (2007). '"We're Nostalgic But We're Not Crazy": Retrofitting the Past in Russia'. *The Russian Review* 66 (3): 451–82.

Oushakine, Serguei Alex. (2013). 'Postcolonial Estrangements: Claiming a Space between Stalin and Hitler'. In *Rites of Place: Public Commemoration in Russia and Eastern Europe*, ed. by Julie A. Buckler and Emily D. Johnson, 285–315. Chicago: Northwestern University Press.

Paperno, Irina. (2011). *Stories of the Soviet Experience: Memoirs, Diaries, Dreams*. Ithaca: Cornell University Press.

Parsons, Talcott. (1965). 'An American Impression of Sociology in the Soviet-Union'. *American Sociological Review* 30 (1): 121–5.

Pinsky, Anatoly, ed. (2018). *Posle Stalina: Pozdnesovetskaia sub'ektivnost' (1953–1985)* (After Stalin: Subjectivity in the Late Soviet Union, 1953–85), 454. St. Petersburg: EUSP Press.

Podsokorsky, Nikolai N. (2020). 'Evoliutsiia Yuriia Dudia: ot populiarnogo videolblogera to obshchestvennogo deiatelia'. *Nauka televideniia* 16 (4): 65–82.

Prokhorova, Irina. (2022). 'Mozhno zakryt' granitsy, no zapretit' dumat' nevozmozhno'. *Skazhi Gordeevoi*. https://www.youtube.com/watch?v=rTwrrqwa0f4

Reddaway, Peter. (2020). *The Dissidents: A Memoir of Working with the Resistance in Russia, 1960–1990*. Washington, DC: Brookings Institution Press.

Reicher, Stephen, S. Alexander Haslam and Nick Hopkins. (2005). 'Social Identity and the Dynamics of Leadership: Leaders and Followers as Collaborative Agents in the Transformation of Social Reality'. *The Leadership Quarterly* 16 (4): 547–68.

Reid, Susan E. (2008). 'Who Will Beat Whom?: Soviet Popular Reception of the American National Exhibition in Moscow, 1959'. *Kritika: Explorations in Russian and Eurasian History* 9 (4): 855–904.

Rogers, Douglas.(2016). *The Old Faith and the Russian Land: A Historical Ethnography of Ethics in the Urals.* Ithaca: Cornell University Press.

Rojansky, Mikhail. (2018). 'Ispytanie Sibir'u: nastoiashchii chelovek na velikikh stroikakh i v fil'makh 1959 goda'. In *Posle Stalina: Pozdnesovetskaia sub'ektivnost' (1953–1985)* (After Stalin: Subjectivity in the Late Soviet Union, 1953–85), 108–44. St. Petersburg: EUSPb Press.

Sandomirskaia, Irina. (2012). 'Naivnoe pis'mo piatnadtsat' let spustia. Ili na smert' avtora'. *Neprikosnovenny zapas:* 2.

Sharafutdinova, Gulnaz. (2019). 'Was There a "Simple Soviet" Person? Debating the Politics and Sociology of 'Homo Sovieticus''. *Slavic Review* 78 (1): 173–95.

Sharafutdinova, Gulnaz. (2020). *The Red Mirror: Putin's Leadership and Russia's Insecure Identity.* New York: Oxford University Press.

Shiller, Robert J., V. Korobov and M. Boycko. (1992). 'Hunting for Homo Sovieticus: Situational Versus Attitudinal Factors in Economic Behavior'. *Brookings Papers on Economic Activity* 1: 127–94.

Shlapentokh, Vladimir. (1989). *Private and Public Life in the Soviet Union: Changing Values in Post-Stalin Russia.* New York: Oxford University Press.

Shlapentokh, Vladimir. (1999). 'The Soviet Union: A Normal Totalitarian Society'. *The Journal of Communist Studies and Transition Politics* 15 (4): 1–16.

Shlapentokh, Vladimir. (2014). *Soviet Intellectuals and Political Power: The Post-Stalin Era.* Princeton: Princeton University Press.

Shlapentokh, Vladimir. (2017). *A Normal Totalitarian Society: How the Soviet Union Functioned and How It Collapsed.* Armonk: Taylor & Francis.

Slezkine, Yuri. (2017). *The House of Government: A Saga of the Russian Revolution.* Princeton: Princeton University Press.

Sokolov, Mikhail. (2017). 'Famous and Forgotten: Soviet Sociology and the Nature of Intellectual Achievement under Totalitarianism'. *Serendipities: Journal for the Sociology and History of the Social Science* 2 (2): 183–212.

Tickner, J. Ann. (2005). 'Gendering a Discipline: Some Feminist Methodological Contributions to International Relations'. *Signs: Journal of Women in Culture and Society* 30 (4): 2173–88.

Titkov, Aleksei. (2019). 'Prizrak sovetskogo cheloveka'. *Sotsiologia vlasti* 4: 53–94.

Tolstoi, Ivan and Andrei Gavrilov. (2018). 'Pervaia kniga Aleksandra Zinovieva'. 29 April 2018. https://www.svoboda.org/a/29194590.html

Tsymbalyuk, Darya. (2022). 'Academia Must Recentre Embodied and Uncomfortable Knowledge'. *Nature Human Behavior,* 19 May 2022.

Turkova, Ksenia. (2021). 'Oktuda vzialos' slovo "sovok"'. 13 December 2021. https://www.golosameriki.com/a/context-istoria-slova-sovok/6352161.html

Tyazhlov, Ivan and Angelina Galanina. (2019). 'A vas ya poproshu izbratsia'. *kommersant.ru*, 21 October 2019. https://www.kommersant.ru/doc/4132969#id1812569.

Tyszka, Krzysztof. (2009). 'Homo Sovieticus Two Decades Later'. *Polish Sociological Review* 168 (4): 507–22.

Vakhstein, Viktor. (2011). 'Post-postsovetskaia sotsiologiia: konets pervogo akta'. *Sotsiologiia: teoriia, Metody, Marketing* (2): 59–77.

Vasil'ev, Sergei. (2018). *Na razlome dvux vremen: 80-e*. Moscow: Alpina Publisher.

Voloshin, Maksimilian. (2018). *Proroki i mstiteli*. Kyiv: Strelbytsky Multimedia Publishing.

Vorozheikina, Tatiana. (2008). 'Tsennostnye ustanovki ili granitsy metoda?' *Vestnik obshchestvennogo mnenia* 4 (96 July–August): 62–9.

Voslensky, Mikhail. (1984). *Nomenklatura: Gospodstvuiushchii klass Sovetskogo Soiuza*. London: Overseas Publication Interchange.

Waldstein, Maxim. (2008). *The Soviet Empire of Signs: A History of the Tartu School of Semiotics*. Saarbrucken: VDM Verlag Dr. Muller.

Warner, Vessela S. (2014). '"Global Dissident": Georgi Markov as a Cold War Playwright and Exile'. *Studia Historica Gedanensia* 2014: 73–94.

Yurchak, Alexei. (2013). *Everything was Forever, Until It Was No More: The Last Soviet Generation*. Princeton: Princeton University Press.

Zaslavsky, Viktor. (1994). *The Neo-Stalinist State: Class, Ethnicity, and Consensus in Soviet Society*. Armonk: Sharpe.

Zaslavsky, Viktor. (2002). 'Postsovetskiy etap izucheniia totalitarizma: novye napravleniia i metodologicheskie tendentsii'. *Monitoring obshchestvennogo mnenia* 1 (57): 45–53.

Zinoviev, Aleksandr. (1979). *The Yawning Heights*. New York: Random House.

Zinoviev, Aleksandr. (1983). *Homo Sovieticus*. Lausanne: L'Âge d'Homme.

Zinoviev, Aleksandr. (1984). *The Reality of Communism*. New York: Schocken Books.

Zinoviev, Aleksandr. (2010). *Nashei Iunosti polet*. AST.

INDEX

Index

Index